DATE DUE

OC 31 '96			
AP 28 '03			
JE 5 03			

Cultivating Intelligence

CRITICAL AMERICA
General Editors: Richard Delgado and Jean Stefancic

White by Law: The Legal Construction of Race
Ian F. Haney López

Cultivating Intelligence: Power, Law, and the Politics of Teaching
Louise Harmon and Deborah W. Post

LOUISE HARMON and DEBORAH W. POST are professors of law at Touro College, Jacob D. Fuchsberg School of Law. LOUISE HARMON has a J.D. from the University of Texas, an L.L.M. from Harvard Law School, and is currently a Ph.D. candidate in philosophy at Columbia University. DEBORAH W. POST is a graduate of Harvard Law School and has studied anthropology at Columbia University, where she was a teaching assistant to Margaret Mead.

Cultivating Intelligence

POWER, LAW, AND THE POLITICS OF TEACHING

A COLLABORATION BY
LOUISE HARMON AND DEBORAH W. POST

NEW YORK UNIVERSITY PRESS

NEW YORK AND LONDON

RSITY PRESS
London

© 1996 by Louise Harmon and Deborah W. Post

Library of Congress Cataloging-in-Publication Data
Harmon, Louise.
Cultivating intelligence : power, law, and the politics of
teaching / a collaboration by Louise Harmon and Deborah W. Post.
p.   cm. — (Critical America)
Includes index.
ISBN 0-8147-6628-5 (cloth : alk. paper). — ISBN 0-8147-6629-3
(pbk. : alk. paper)
1. Law—Study and teaching—United States.   2. Academic freedom—
United States.   3. Afro-American women law teachers—Anecdotes.
I. Post, Deborah W.   II. Title.   III. Series.
KF273.H266   1996
340'.071'1—dc20   95-32500
CIP

New York University Press books are printed on acid-free paper,
and their binding materials are chosen for strength and durability.

Book design by Jennifer Dossin

Manufactured in the United States of America

1 3 5 7 9 10 8 6 4 2

THIS BOOK IS DEDICATED TO OUR CHILDREN
CHRISTOPHER DUBOIS TRAVIS
AND
NAN, KATE, AND JOHANNA JORDAN.

CONTENTS

Spring
PLANTING THE SEEDS AND GERMINATION

Summer
RAIN AND SHINE AND GROWTH

Contents

Fall
BEFORE THE FROST

Winter
SITTING AROUND THE FIRE

ACKNOWLEDGMENTS

We would like to thank our friend Hazel Weiser who made invaluable comments on the first draft of the manuscript. We would also like to thank Richard Delgado and Jean Stefancic. We are deeply indebted to them for their enthusiasm and support and for convincing us that we had written a book.

We would also like to thank Amelia Wilson for providing invaluable assistance in getting the book ready for publication, Lynn Oatman for keeping the lines of international communication open, and our research assistants, Daphna Zekaria, Deborah Conquest, and Brad Hammock—all of whom seem to have energy and organizational skills that surpass our own. We would also like to thank our colleagues Andy Herz and Marjorie Silver for their reflections on the retreat, and the staff of the Touro Law Library who found what we needed when we needed it.

We are grateful to Touro College, Jacob D. Fuchsberg

School of Law, and our beloved dean, Howard A. Glickstein, for the summer research grants. We are also grateful to the Gonzaga University School of Law Institute for Law School Teaching for its financial assistance and to Gerald F. Hess, the director, and Paula Prather, the administrator, for their infinite patience. Points of view expressed in the book are those of the authors and do not necessarily reflect the positions or policies of the Institute for Law School Teaching.

The graph for plotting disciplines is adapted by permission of A. Biglan and the American Psychological Association, from "The Characteristics of Subject Matter in Different Academic Areas," by A. Biglan, © 1973 by the American Psychological Association.

The diagram depicting the dialectical process of learning is reprinted by permission of David A. Kolb and Jossey-Bass, Inc., from "Learning Styles and Disciplinary Differences," Figure 1, by David A. Kolb, *The Modern American College: Responding to the New Realities of Diverse Students in a Changing Society,* edited by A. W. Chickering and Associates, © 1981 Jossey-Bass, Inc., Publishers.

Deborah wants to thank her colleagues in law teaching who generously tolerate her attempts at auto-ethnography even when they dispute the meaning she assigns to the events in which they were participants. Louise wants to thank her helpmate, Daniel P. Jordan, Jr., for his continued support and affection. We both want to thank our students for providing us with the stories that form the basis of this book and for giving us a reason for caring about its ideas.

LOUISE'S PROLOGUE

Deborah, it keeps happening to me: my expectations get in the way. I start a project with preconceived ideas about how things are going to turn out, and then they don't. Something different happens. I think it is going to be a gardening project, and being a dutiful reader of instructive books, I turn over the rocks in preparation of the soil. Underneath those rocks, I fall in love with the scurrying creatures whose peace and pressure I have disturbed, those green iridescent beetles, and those shy shell-less mottled mollusks, shrinking from the sun and aridity. I put the rocks back, gently, reverently, and wish that I had brought a different instructive book—one about life in the darkness under a rock, and not about the glory of a flower bed doomed from the start.

I curse the clumsy gloves on my hands, I kick the bag of fertilizer with all that redundant dirt, I toss my trowel, a bulldozer of a tool, ill-equipped to tackle any task of delicacy. For me, it is not really a matter of disappointment. After all, this has happened to me enough times not to be a surprise, and from experience I know that I will not only survive, but benefit from these seismic shifts in interest and passion. It is more a matter of profound annoyance, that I should be sitting on a stool in the grass with the wrong book, the wrong tools, and the wrong set of questions— but they caught me unawares, those scurrying creatures with their utter panic at exposure.

For a long time, though, the very thought of flowers drove me to distraction. I saw them in my dreams, and when I shut my eyes in waking sleep, profuse explosions of fuchsia, phlox, petunias, peonies, and lobelia, purples and violet blues, smashing yellows and deep, deep reds, all floated on that river of pulsating darkness. I could not give them up, my floral fantasies, the image of how things were going to turn out, inspired by pictures on packages of seeds that were never opened. My pitiful expectations kept getting in the way.

A year ago, when we decided to explore cognitive theory, I had expectations that we would all read together, and learn about how people learn, and that this would make us better teachers. I thought those were modest expectations, but one year later, still unfulfilled, they have acquired a grotesque grandeur. I sought in vain for the right metaphor to capture the essence of the failure: abortion, extirpation, death by drought. None of them worked, since all implied germination.

But I have since settled into our failure. I like it here in the grass. I like knowing there is something alive and fascinating under those rocks. Deborah, is it OK with you if we throw the seeds away?

DEBORAH'S PROLOGUE

Louise, don't throw out the seeds, put them aside. Your question reminds me of my cousin M'Lynn. It's the kind of question she would ask. You both have this habit of turning an idea, plans for the future, an act of imagining, into something concrete. This idea, this plan, this image of a flower garden grabbed hold of you and won't let go.

M'Lynn does the same thing. Listening to us talk, you might think that of the two of us, M'Lynn is the one who most resembles an unreconstructed flower child. She lives in Colorado and, from time to time, she has been known to make reference to requests she makes of "the universe." But if the image of a flower child in the popular imagination is an airhead, M'Lynn is the antithesis of that image. When it comes to life she is—well, disciplined is the word I would choose. M'Lynn is extremely thorough in her planning— the only person I know who can tell you what her vacation plans are two years in advance. And I drive her crazy because she thinks I don't plan enough; or that I do not have the proper appreciation of the imperatives of time.

One year, when M'Lynn was with me in New York, about six different disasters occurred just as we were about to leave town to visit our relatives upstate. I resolved most of the problems, made the necessary adjustments, changed the date of departure, cut out one leg of the trip, and we still managed to enjoy ourselves. It was the first time I remember her expressing admiration for me rather than disapproval.

M'Lynn admitted that it would have been difficult for her to do what I had done. She thought it amazing that I could juggle so many things at one time, that I could keep track of so many different strands of my life. But most of all, I think she was surprised at her own reaction to the changes. She could live with things not happening the way we had planned. Of course, she was not in control, and so she was absolved of responsibility. Freed from responsibility, she could relax and enjoy whatever happened. She could even appreciate the advantages of a different philosophy of life, my philosophy—all plans are contingent and no plan is ever completely abandoned.

If there were a test that measured something called the "guilt factor," I think I would score pretty high. But one of the many things I don't feel guilty about is altering my course midstream. I have difficulty understanding why you would choose to describe what has happened to us as a failure. How can a decision not to do something, or a decision that you can't do something *right now* be a failure?

Both you and M'Lynn apologize for changing plans as if you have been found wanting in some deep way, as though this were a reflection on your character and your moral worth.

The only constraint on our future plans, and the only possible source of regret, would be our failure to meet the expectations we have created in others. And we do have someone to whom we have made representations, someone to whom we owe something. You can't decide not to plant a flower garden after someone buys the seeds for you, and then opens a flower shop in anticipation of a bumper crop of carnations.

But would he mind a slight delay? There is more than one planting season, even in the space of a single year, and seeds don't spoil, at least not right away. A flower garden is one of those things that can be deferred—your dreams become a promise, an expression of your hope, not a measure of disappointment.

Patience and unexpected events sometimes conspire to give us much more than we bargained for. He might applaud our decision to observe the invisible world of iridescent green beetles and shy shell-less mottled mollusks.

So, Louise, let's hang on to the seeds. The only thing facing us now is time and unexamined possibilities.

Spring

PLANTING
THE
SEEDS
AND
GERMINATION

ONE

Spring

TILLING
THE SOIL:
CONFESSIONS
OF A
FIRST-YEAR
LAW TEACHER

Do you remember last year, Deborah, when in a fit of organization I discovered the fragments of an essay I had written during my first year of teaching? It was that confrontation with my former self which really started this gardening project.

Cleaning off my desk is like performing an archaeological dig. As I work through the piles I move backward in time, peeling back the layers of history until I hit Formica.

During the excavation I found an unfinished essay tucked away in an unmarked file. It was entitled "Some Thoughts on My First Year of Law Teaching." Dated 1984, it was full of ancient trauma about crippling nausea and fear of questions I could not answer. The essay was also full of chronic worry about what I was supposed to be doing. A decade later, I find that many of those concerns are still painfully present. Here is an excerpt:

> During all of the first semester of my first year of teaching and a good part of the second, I was frequently on the verge of throwing up. It was the worst right before class, when I would be seized by anxiety over whether I knew the material. I would scan the case one more time, and words usually familiar suddenly became alien. The procedural context of the case, which had seemed simple and straightforward the night before, suddenly assumed a Byzantine complexity. Often, just minutes before I entered the classroom, I would think of one question about the material that I did not know the answer to, and would fantasize—not only that a student would ask it, but that Irene Brunstein would have the answer, and I would not. Irene Brunstein was an incredibly bright woman in my Property class who had nothing else to do with her life but think of questions I did not know the answer to. I should have bought stock in Procter & Gamble for all the Pepto-Bismol I imbibed.
>
> I was the only woman teacher added to the fac-

ulty last year, and when I confessed my constant state of nausea to my male colleagues, also new teachers, they all seemed surprised. I can still remember my friend, Gary Shaw, telling me to relax, that "all teachers enjoy a presumption of competence." I know now that he was wrong: all male teachers enjoy a presumption of competence. There is another presumption in operation for women teachers, one that justifies my anxiety.

At my first law teaching conference, I went to the University of Texas reception and ran into my Business Organizations teacher, Robert Hamilton. I did not know him well, and doubt that he remembered my name, but he politely asked me how my first year of law teaching was going. For some reason, I blurted out that I wanted to throw up all the time. I felt like a real fool. I hardly knew the man, and here I was confessing my addiction to Pepto-Bismol. At the very least, I expected a version of the presumption of competence; at the worst, that he was going to tell me to give up on teaching. But he didn't. He looked at me in that intense, intelligent furry mammal way he has, head cocked to the side, knuckles popping, and nodding knowingly, said, "If you still feel like throwing up all the time in a year from now, you might want to get out of teaching."

That was all he said. His implicit words of wisdom, that time would probably take care of the problem, turned out to be true. As the months roll by, some of my more primitive, visceral fears about teaching begin to fade. I am still in the clutches of a cycle of dread and elation, and still prone to sporadic nausea, but the level of panic has begun to diminish. Once my body became accustomed to the jolt of performing every day, my mind took advantage of the physical security to ask disturbing questions. There is one umbrella disturbing question under which all others found shelter: What is it exactly I am supposed to be doing?

My goals in teaching law were, and to a large extent still are, amorphous things, murky and subterranean. It amazed me that no one at the law school ever bothered to inquire before I started teaching whether I knew what I was doing or why I was doing it. Presumably this unwarranted confidence in my instant expertise had something to do with the ridiculous criteria by which we select new law teachers. High class rank, the right law school, and some indicia of honor like law review: those were the only credentials needed to start teaching in a law school.

Personally, I see little or no relationship between being a good teacher and having accumulated a high grade point average at a prestigious school. The credentials are only instrumental in getting you the job in the first place, but having the right stuff on your résumé does not guarantee success once you have entered the classroom. A new law teacher is a poor naked thing, stripped of visible symbols of achievement, and totally devoid of any qualifications for the task at hand: education. And women law teachers are even more naked, if there can be degrees of nakedity. We lack the right body type, the right secondary sexual characteristics, the right posture, the right clothes, the right voice, the right sense of humor, the right point of view.

I am told that this sink or swim mentality with respect to law teaching is a time honored tradition in legal education. Time may honor it, but I do not.

I may have already told you, Deborah, that I unearthed the yellowed pages of this essay on the same day that I found the call for grant proposals from the Institute for Law Teaching in my mailbox. I took both to you at lunch, and we laughed over my nausea, and my clumsy words— in particular whether there was such a word as "na-kedity"—and then we bemoaned, as we so often do, our ignorance about learning and teaching, and about the relationship between the two. I would not say that we planted any seeds that day, but we did stir up the ground.

And so I wrote the grant proposal, a by-product of that conversation and those unanswered questions from many years ago. They were not really my questions, but came from the collective unconscious that manifests itself in unfinished essays tucked away in unmarked files. They belong to us all, to anyone who has ever walked into a classroom and not had the privilege of sitting down.

In the proposal, I asked for a grant to pay someone who had expertise in cognitive theory to speak at a law school faculty retreat. This expert in education would compile a bibliography and help prepare selected background materials for our colleagues to read. We were going to ask our colleagues to venture into a new discipline, to explore what educators had to say about how people learn—and perhaps, about how we should teach. You and I, Deborah, were going to experiment with new teaching strategies, encouraging our colleagues to do the same. Finally, we were going to collaborate on a piece of writing about applying cognitive theory to law school teaching—something brilliant and insightful.

Thus spake the packet of seeds.

Spring

TILLING
MORE SOIL:
CONFESSIONS
OF A
CURRENT LAW
PROFESSOR

Louise, I have a confession to make. This research is about vindication. I know it's dangerous to begin a project with the hope and expectation that my own beliefs will be vindicated, but that's what this research is all about. Self-affirmation is seductive.

When I read about your nausea, I thought at first that you were describing something I would call performance anxiety. Performance anxiety diminishes with time, although the memory of that anxiety is replayed physically before each class as a mild case of jitters or butterflies in the stomach. Performance anxiety is frivolous when compared to the deeper and more disturbing questions you raise: your doubts about the way we do what we do and about the worth of it. My doubts, like yours, are recurrent, like some perennial that I planted once and forgot about, and which surprises me each year when it sprouts and flowers again.

Your anxiety is not as long-standing as mine, even though we have been in teaching for the same amount of time. I am not saying this to be competitive, though I often feel we are competing, even when you deny it. This is just a statement about the different places from which our shared experience of doubt originate.

I began to notice when I was in practice, and then later in teaching, that there were certain white women—not all, but some—who never seemed to have any doubts. Their confidence in their own worth was striking, given the reasonableness of some degree of insecurity in the face of open resentment of women. These white women thought they understood the rules, and generally they were very successful, at least until that day when some man or group of men denied them something to which they believed they were entitled. I generally associate this confidence on the part of white women professionals with privilege, with women whose egos have been wrapped in tissue paper and placed in a protected crevice between white privilege and class privilege.

That sounds unkind, but it is not meant that way. You

may joke about your "downward mobility," you may despise your white Southern grandmother whose aristocratic airs were almost as offensive as her racism, but there are incidental benefits to status which you don't even notice. It is a presumption of competence that is internal, not external.

And that is why I was surprised at your fear and your anxiety about teaching—surprised and pleased. Isn't that perverse? It is a comfort to know that we can talk about these issues. I now know you will understand the feelings of anger and fear and uncertainty that alternate with the sense of satisfaction I sometimes experience when I walk out of the classroom. You will understand my periodic anxiety attacks.

Have I ever mentioned the reaction of a friend, Bisa Manigault, whom I expected to be overjoyed at my announcement that I was leaving practice to enter law teaching? She was teaching Spanish and Portuguese at Rice University. My news shocked her. I could read her reaction on her face. The comment she blurted out was negative as well, a judgment about the arrogance of my profession which I experienced as a judgment about me personally. "What makes lawyers assume they can teach?" Her question described my lack of qualifications, and like you, I was forced to ask myself exactly what I knew about teaching law.

When you suggested we apply for this grant, I heard Bisa's words echo in my mind again. But for the first time in a long time, I felt I might have an answer to her accusation and my uncertainty. Here is a chance to have someone who has experience, someone other than a law school teacher, someone whose opinions are informed by real knowledge about the way people learn and the way we teach, tell me that I am going about this the right way, that the choices I have made over the years are the correct ones. At the beginning of this enterprise, I feel the intellectual equivalent of gravity in the ideals of neutrality and the scientific method. I want someone who knows something about teaching to give me an answer.

Over the years, I have developed my own teaching theories. As usual, my son, Christopher, provided me with a story I can use as a partial explanation of my approach and my struggle and my frustration as a teacher. He came home one day and told me about an examination he took in his English class. The students were being tested, he thought, to determine their personality types.[1] Initials were used to describe these personality types, but he couldn't remember what the initials were. He tried to describe for me some of the characteristics associated with the various types, and he began by contrasting the responses he observed.

The students, all ninth-graders in the local high school, were asked to describe the ideal learning environment, the perfect classroom. Chris and several other students came up with descriptions that emphasized informality. Theirs was a classroom in which students sat around on sofas and easy chairs and instruction took the form of extended conversations with their classmates and the teacher. Chris and his compatriots in what I will now and forever more think of as the "couch and conversation" style learning group were shocked to learn that other students preferred a classroom with desks. Not only did those students want desks; they wanted desks in rows. They wanted a teacher in the front of the class and they wanted a system (using cubbyholes or boxes) for collecting and distributing homework assignments.

As Christopher's paternal grandmother, Agnes, would say, this preference for conversation is something Chris comes by "naturally"; it is a preference he shares with his mother. I am a "couch and conversation" style teacher in a room with 106 students in neat little rows, many of whom want me to say important things in a way that is compatible with an outline format for recording information. I have come to expect the pilgrimage to the front of the class or to my office on those days when, for the sake of expediency or because I want to spend some time on another issue, I lecture. The students come up to tell me how good that class was, as though they think that a little positive reinforcement will make me mend my ways.

The dichotomy that Chris described is almost too neat, but it works well as a metaphor for the consequences of my pedagogical choices, the kind of struggle I feel is occurring inside and outside the classroom. From the very beginning, I experienced teaching as a battle of wills.

I know that credibility is part of the problem. I am suffering from some sort of pedagogical deficiency attributable to my status as a Black woman, the counterpoint to Gary Shaw's presumption of competence. This is not just some individual psychosis, some form of paranoia—unless it is a collective paranoia.[2] Far too many Black women teachers have confirmed my experience. Patricia Williams's stories are probably the best known,[3] but I think Regina Austin provided the most compelling and succinct description of our lived experience as teachers when she wrote in her article "Sapphire Bound!" "Black Bitch Hunts are alive and well in legal academia."[4] It sounds intemperate, a statement like that, but what is the point of describing in elegant and genteel terms something as ugly as the public attacks on Pat and Regina or Lani Guinier and Anita Hill?

I am feeling pretty Sapphirish myself these days when I think about my alma mater and its treatment of Black women. How many years has it been since Harvard adopted the rule that would not allow the faculty to consider Regina Austin for a tenure-track position while she was visiting there? Coincidentally, the next year, when white males were visiting, the rule was abandoned. If I accused Harvard of hypocrisy and deceit, the representatives of that august institution would proclaim their innocent intent. "We didn't mean what it would be reasonable for you to understand we meant" is an absolute defense to charges of racism and sexism these days.

Those who believe that Harvard does not intentionally discriminate probably also believe that Harvard cannot find a Black woman who is qualified for the job. I hear there is a list of women with whom the powers that be may negotiate. These women have made the *short* list of potential candidates. If you haven't figured it out yet, the list is short because at Harvard the only "qualified" Black woman is one who already has a national reputation. While the institution is willing to take a risk on men whom they hire for entry-level positions—nurturing or mentoring aspiring teachers and scholars, including several Black men—it still has not been able to find *one* qualified Black woman to hire in an entry-level tenure-track position.

But this project of ours is not about the credibility of Black women, so I will have to put that aside for the moment. There is something else I want to describe here, something very basic about this struggle I am having with my students. I want the study of law to be part of "the interminable journey of the human mind."[5] I have chosen conversation as the vehicle for our journey, but my students want no part of it.

The great thing about conversation is that it roams around. There are innumerable occasions for digression in conversations; innumerable occasions to point out the connections between ideas and have the connections that others see revealed to you. I want to explore the nooks and crannies of the law. Why do I feel I have to catch students off guard, cajoling and teasing them, or confronting them in a way that expresses the power of my position, to get them to accompany me on this journey?

A few years ago, Louise, you suggested that they might have problems with my discursive style, the syntax of my answers to students' questions, the way I think out loud in the classroom. Some students do seem to have a problem following my lead.

My sister Naomi complained recently that I never answer a question with a simple "no" or "yes." The complaint was occasioned by my response to her question, "Do you have American cheese?" I began my answer with "I have luncheon meat" and proceeded to describe the contents of my refrigerator. She was exasperated and I was surprised.

You see, I heard her question and interpreted it to mean, "I want to feed your nephew, Akeem, who is six and likes American cheese." What was the point of saying, "No. I have no cheese," and then waiting for her to ask, "Well, what have you got?"

I may be guilty of the same sort of transgression in my teaching. I might occasionally answer unarticulated questions, anticipating the logic of a particular line of reasoning. For those who like to see things laid out, step by step, this can be disconcerting. But this is not a right-hand turn or a digression of any kind. I am still on the same path; I have just sprinted ahead.

But I admit I have also been guilty of making the occasional mental left-hand turn without signaling. On those occasions, I can hear my students march past me, compelled by inertia, or by logic or by a physical or emotional commitment to the march itself. They are on their way to the gardening store to stock up on fertilizer and tools and I, like you, have made a detour to look at iridescent beetles.

I admit that it is not as important to me as it may be to my students to know where I am at all times. I have stopped to figure out what the beetles have to do with the texture or quality of the soil and what effect they will have on the flower I am about to plant. Will we, as you assume, wreak havoc with the ecosystem, or will the beetles rejoice in the scent and the vision of the flower?

A student came by to see me the other day. He claimed he had not been so confused since his first year of law school. I pressed him to get at the reason for his confusion. He finally concluded that it was the manner in which the conversation in the classroom proceeded, the combination of levels of discourse, the mixing of the real and the ideal— what the law is; what the law could be; what the law should be.

There are certain kinds of questions that have this effect—questions that cannot be answered in one hour, in one classroom, or sometimes in an entire legal career. Questions like these remain in the classroom in some sort of intellectual suspended animation long after they have been asked. And if more than one is asked, even if they are asked at different points in the classroom discussion, students' experience is one of simultaneity.

I like this student. I like his honesty and I appreciate his interest in what I see as a collaborative undertaking, a learning experience. I find it hard to reconcile myself to the "loss" of a student, and yet I know that I lose a few every year. For instance, I know that there is another man in my class whom I have no hope of reaching. I don't think I can bridge the gap that divides me from the first-year law student who analogized law to a shoe factory. Shoe factories make shoes, he argued, because it is hard to walk around without them. Legislatures and courts make laws because it is hard to live without them. He has little tolerance for history, philosophy, or politics.

This student focuses on what he considers the practical questions that occupy "real" lawyers. A few years ago, I would have imagined myself closer to him than to legal scholars who occupy themselves with the theories of continental philosophers. I came to teaching from practice, with the desire and the expectation that I would teach my students those things they would need to know as practitioners.

Both of us have been in teaching long enough now to witness one or more of the recurrent struggles over control between academics and practitioners. When we enter a period of reexamination (read criticism), the profession, represented by the American Bar Association, usually takes academics to task. What is at issue is our ability to prepare our students for the practice of law.[6] The most recent evaluation is called the MacCrate Report, issued in 1992 by the ABA Task Force on Law Schools and the Profession.[7] The report uses the variety of settings in which lawyers work today to represent in some gross way the differences in legal tasks and problems.[8] After acknowledging the difficulty in maintaining a "unitary concept of being a lawyer," the report then describes the skills and values that lawyers need.

The MacCrate Report adopts a code-like approach to organize its conclusions, listing ten skills and four values, with lots of subsets in both classes. When I first entered teaching, I had a similar approach. I assumed that there were certain basic skills all lawyers should have. All lawyers need to know how to read a statute; they need to be familiar with the principles of the common law; they need to know the areas of controversy in a field of law, the battles being waged in courts and in the law journals; they need to know how to draft a document. If I had to find one way to describe or summarize all these tasks, I would say law students need to learn how to advise and how to solve a client's legal problems.

When I taught in Texas, I could ask former colleagues from the law firm where I worked to collaborate on projects. I used their war stories to construct hypotheticals. They lent credibility to our enterprise; they persuaded the students that the material we covered was relevant to life after law school.

Over a period of ten years, my practice experience became remote and the ideology of the law more immediate. I found myself wondering why my students did not see certain issues, why they could not imagine using a particular doctrine to solve a problem. I began to question how my students think about the law, what they see when they read a case.

I still consider my courses "skills" courses, even though I have stopped assigning projects. I no longer ask my students to prepare articles of incorporation or pleadings or office memoranda; there are no more projects that simulate a practice experience. I have justified this decision to myself by acknowledging the existence of upper-level drafting courses and specialized seminars, the existence of clinics and externships where students have the opportunity to represent clients. I tell myself that first-year students have their hands full with the legal writing course. I do not need to add to that burden.

I hope I am teaching a different skill. I want them to think about the relevance of their own values and beliefs to practice; I want them to understand that practice necessarily includes political *and* moral choices. I want them to consider what justice means and to understand the imperatives of justice. We don't talk about justice often enough in law school anymore; we refer to it euphemistically as public policy.[9] I don't want them to go through their professional lives thinking "public policy" is political and not moral. I am not alone in my desire to make these choices explicit. Many of my colleagues who some call "outsiders," women and people of color, gays and lesbians, among others, consider the revelation of unstated but powerful assumptions underlying doctrine and theory an important educational objective. And we are accused of teaching something other than law because we do.[10]

The criticism I receive from students is sometimes fueled by fear and at other times by anger. Resistance takes different forms in different students and varies at different points in the academic year. Second- and third-year students are more intolerant of theory than the first-year students I teach. One or two years into the program, they have defined their educational goals in a very specific way. They want to receive the information they will need to pass the bar examination. If I cannot persuade my students that ideas are worth exploring, that law school is an intellectual journey worthwhile in and of itself, it is because many of them want to follow the most direct route to what they see as their immediate objective. They are seeking within the domain of the law the equivalent of the Seven Cities of Gold, a job with one of the Wall Street law firms.[11]

Wall Street works well as a metaphor. It has become a symbol of achievement, wealth, and prestige within the legal profession. For law students, the prestige of corporate practice is proved by the decision of Wall Street law firms to hire only the "outstanding" graduates of top-tier law schools at very high salaries and with the promise of partnership after a probationary period that we all know as the "partnership track." Scarcity and exclusivity usually can be relied on to increase value. For students of small or medium-sized law schools, schools we label "regional," the prestige that attaches to a job offer at a Wall Street firm is heady stuff.

As the MacCrate Report points out, the law has been viewed as the most unequal of all the professions in the incomes of its members, and since the 1970s the inequality has become increasingly more severe.[12] When I read this statement in the MacCrate Report, I couldn't figure out whose view was being referenced. It can't be prelaw students in most undergraduate schools or our entering students. I am not sure law students really understand the significance of this inequality until they start applying for jobs. Law students from the smaller and regional schools are the persons in the job market who are most likely to enter into solo practice because of the lack of other options. The difference between their expectations when they applied to law school and the financial hardship of solo practice is one measure of the inequality within the profession.

If the life of a law school teacher has become more difficult in recent years, it is because the Wall Street job has proven to be as inaccessible as those mythical cities of gold. In their disillusionment, some of our students have become surly and militant.

Sometimes I suspect that students might have fewer problems with politics or philosophy or history if I gave them the "right" kind of theories, the laissez-faire version of law and economics, the kind of theory they could use to impress Wall Street lawyers. They could follow me if they chose to, but they just don't like the direction I'm headed in. They are not interested in the ideas about race, gender, and class that I find in the rhetoric of decisions or in the way courts or lawmakers or students think about particular legal problems. Their complaint that theory is irrelevant is really a way of saying that my theories are suspect. Anything I give them to read must be "propaganda" for a way of thinking with which they disagree.

Last year in Business Organizations, I assigned a law review article that discussed the issue we were covering, the difference between an independent contractor and an employee, in an unusual way. The textbook has cases which talk about issues of liability—does an agent have authority to bind a principal? Is the agent an employee or an independent contractor? The article I assigned discussed the relevance of a person's status as employee or independent contractor to the protections offered by federal labor laws. At issue was the right of farm workers to a minimum wage and the protection of the child labor laws.

My judgment about the importance and relevance of this issue is experiential. It can be traced to my childhood in upstate New York. Migrant workers passed through Auburn on their way to Kings Ferry and other adjacent communities to pick crops like string beans and peas. As a child, I was aware that the living conditions on those farms were abominable. The circumstances of the migrant workers were real to me and to other members of the Black community. Every year, a few families would stay behind when everyone else traveled south, looking for jobs or electing to receive public assistance rather than work for less than the cost of living, making a choice they hoped would improve their lives and the lives of their children.

We were cruel to the children of those migrant workers. We taunted them and called them "bean pickers," a name that set up an opposition between those of us who were second- or third-generation Auburnians, descendants of the original settlers or passengers on the Underground Railroad, and the new residents. Any work our family had done in the fields was remote. The name we chose for the newest residents of our town branded them outsiders, uneducated, poor. While we might count ourselves among the aristocracy in the Black community, we knew we were at the bottom of the social ladder in our small town. We were afraid to be associated with people who were so much like the stereotypes of Black people we were trying desperately to live down. My Aunt Dorothy likes to point out that there were many among the "aristocracy" who could have learned something about motivation, self-improvement and ambition from those Southern immigrants. But you can't learn from those you have isolated, stigmatized, ridiculed.

That was my experience with migrant workers. I wonder whether it is also the experience of my students, many of whom are natives of Long Island. I know that Long Island, at least the East End, is also an agricultural community. Even here, closer to Manhattan, we drive past fields planted with cash crops and truck farms on our way to the Long Island Expressway. Why don't we notice the people who harvest the crops? I decided to make farm workers visible by assigning an article that described the way the law affects the quality of their lives. The article was called "Harvest of Shame," a title obviously borrowed from the famous television documentary.[13]

I asked my students to write a short essay, a "reflection piece" in which they discussed their reaction to the article. Students will sometimes say in an essay what they will not say in class, and I learn a lot about the problems students have with my teaching from reading these essays. One student wrote:

> At first glance, A Harvest of Shame succeeds in what it sets out to do. It stirs up an emotional response from its readers by painting a heart rending picture of young children standing amidst huge crops sprayed with poisonous chemicals and working their tiny fingers to the bone. It was not until my third reading of the article that I began to form a more objective view of this problem and it was one that was quite different than my first instinct had caused me to form.
>
> The first time I read this piece, a familiar scene came to mind. . . . It reminded me of the kitchen help my father has in his restaurant. . . . Their hours are long, the heat is unbearable, and while the money is not bad, they will never be rich. . . . While their jobs do not appear all that exciting to me, the workers truly seem to be satisfied. . . .
>
> I for one have faith in our court system, unlike

Ms. Glader who refers to those who do not agree
with her as racist. Perhaps Jeanne Glader would see
me as a racist too when I tell her that she must be
realistic in evaluating situations such as those. We
live in a capitalistic society, not socialist or commu-
nist. Legal loopholes exist, such as the one that
exists in the FLSA which allows children to work on
"family farms." The farm owners should not be the
ones who carry the full burden of blame. They are
running their farms within the constraints of the
law. It is the parents who are allowing the children
to work. The farm owners are not going out and
signing seven year old children to work contracts.

It may be unfortunate, but the farm owner knows
that if one family does not want the job, there are
many others who do. My father is aware of this
reality and while it appears harsh on the surface,
this is how our society operates.[14]

This student is angry at the accusation of racism leveled
at those who are insensitive to the plight of farm workers,
and she is not alone in this sentiment.

I am bothered by the way my students use empirical
evidence to prove their point. The distance between the
student who authored this reflection piece and me is not
political; it is cognitive. How is it that she feels how unbear-
ably hot the kitchen is, experiences how unrewarding the
work is, how low the pay is, but concludes that the workers
are truly satisfied? She sees a legal regime that allows the
use of loopholes, and I see a moral issue that has not been

adequately addressed by the law. We are not on opposite sides of an ideological divide, socialists on one side, capitalists on the other. We are on opposite sides of a cognitive divide. We do not interpret "facts," we do not see the world, in the same way. I feel compelled to write a long, long response to each of the points she raises, which she accepts with a smile and no comment.

Over the years, I have developed my own definition of good teaching. I have learned to live with the contradictions and the consequences of my choices. I know that my choice of teaching style, my self-conscious "couch and conversation" style of teaching, is an expression of my commitment to a particular ideology. I am willing to put these choices to the test because of the doubt that nags at me from time to time. I have made myself a promise that this research and the book that comes from it will be about teaching and only teaching, not merely about cultural preferences, gender, race, and class.

You say that I am a closet modernist, someone who believes in truth.[15] I suppose you are right, Louise, for if I didn't believe in truth, there would be no reason for me to care about honesty. And I do care about honesty. So in the interest of truth and honesty, I am confessing that my motive in joining you in this project is, at least in part, a desire to justify my own convictions about teaching and my choices with respect to teaching techniques and style.

Summer

RAIN
AND
SHINE
AND
GROWTH

THREE

Summer

THE FIRST DAY OF THE RETREAT

Here we are, Deborah: it is time to sit down and write this thing. My job is to tell the story of the faculty retreat, its form and substance. It is not an easy task. For one thing, it requires me to conjure up a brutally cold winter day, when last night it was so sweltering that we had to let all three girls sleep on the floor of our air-conditioned bedroom. Today, as I sit at the computer and think about writing, I can see waves of heat rising from the almost empty parking lot of the law school. I am hot, and crabby, and snow and ice are only concepts: words that do not refer.

I am also crabby for other reasons. Writing this thing forces me to face some failures about the project and myself. If we had not promised Gerry Hess and the Institute for Law School Teaching to produce a manuscript, I would gladly remain in the oral tradition. We could just talk the thing out—how we had great plans for the faculty retreat and for the faculty's active participation in learning and experimenting with cognitive theory—and the project could die a quick, dignified death. It is so hot, you and I could just go outside and sit under the parking lot tree, and dictate into the air. Our words would evaporate over the asphalt, into that shimmering, wobbly lower atmosphere, and then we could give up on the garden altogether and go to the pool.

So where do I start? Maybe with the story of how we found Lee Knefelkamp, our consultant on cognitive theory and speaker for the first day of the retreat. We got her name when we were in Boston at a conference on Critical Legal Everything. When we got the brochure for the conference, I remember saying to you how much I wanted to go, and how maybe I could see Linda Fentiman and Arthur Levine, and how Arthur might know someone in education who could speak at our retreat.[1] But I was postpartum. Johanna was only three weeks old, just a sweet sack of potatoes, and there was no way I could go. Then you said with the gusto that only someone who has forgotten what babies are like can say, "Oh, we can go. We'll bring the baby!" Your idea was that we would take turns with Johanna, each of us attending different sessions. She was so little, all she ever did was curl up in the Snuglie and snurfle and sleep. She wouldn't be any trouble. It would be fun.

And of course it would have been fun if we had attended the conference the very same day. Unfortunately, the conference was six weeks later, and in the meantime Johanna had learned to lift her head and look around—to find another set of human eyes and disarm them with a smile. She was no longer content to lie there like a lump in the Snuglie. Instead, her head poked out of the top, right under my chin, like a turtle, except that unlike a turtle who seems content with his view, Johanna kept trying to negotiate a different one. She found the conference stimulating. She never slept.

I took her to one session, and had to leave after five minutes. My plan had been to sneak in late and slide into the back row; no one would even notice that I had a sweet sack of potatoes on my chest. But the session that I attended was held in a classroom in which the only door was located several feet away from the blackboard. Not only that—and this I should have anticipated—the leaders of the session hoped to make a statement against hierarchy by having all the attendees sit in a circle. I hate sitting in a circle. Even without having a fourteen-pound, wiggling, drooling infant strapped to my chest, I hate sitting in a circle. Give me hierarchy any day, as long as I get to sit in the back row.

But at least I got to see Linda and Arthur. Why didn't you come to dinner with me that night, Deborah? I can't remember. I know that you were invited, but you must have had other plans; you always have other plans. Waiting for Arthur, Linda and I drank wine in their kitchen and ruminated on the meaning of life after tenure. Johanna, exhausted from her charm fest in the hallways, slept in the carseat that we had dragged out of the back seat in the rain. When Arthur came home, he cooked dinner, and during the course of the conversation, I asked Arthur who would be a good speaker for a faculty retreat about teaching and learning in law school.

We met Lee Knefelkamp several months later, you and I and Peter Zablotsky upon whose shoulders the organization of the retreat had fallen.[2] It was one of those brilliant early June days, which made the contrast between the brightness of the Manhattan streets and the dimness of the cavernous corridors of Teachers College so stark. The air is grey inside Teachers College, probably because no one has opened the windows for decades. (I am not even sure there are windows in Teachers College.) It is still possible to catch a cold from John Dewey who has been dead for over forty years.

After waiting outside her office for some time, we finally got to talk to Lee Knefelkamp. She is a pleasant woman, about my age, and she seemed to really like you, Deborah, and Peter. I don't think she much liked me, but she was genial and helpful. She would be happy to send us materials for distribution to our colleagues during the semester before the retreat, to provide us with a bibliography on cognitive theory and adult learning, and to be our presenter at the retreat. We discussed nothing substantive, only logistics such as time and place and consideration.

The meeting was cordial and brief, and in no time, the three of us found ourselves on the corner of 120th and Broadway, blinded by the sun of the twentieth century. We chatted about the interview, and the possibility of lunch, and I wondered to myself how this businesslike, low-key woman was going to project in the pedagogical arena; it was hard to imagine that she was the star Arthur promised her to be.

The next semester, we waited and waited for the materials. Finally, in almost the last week of classes, Lee Knefelkamp express-mailed us a packet of articles on cognitive theory to select for our colleagues to read. It was too late for leisurely consumption of the materials: the retreat was in ten days. Because of the Thanksgiving holiday, we ran into a copying and binding crunch, and we ended up doing everything ourselves. All semester, she had been impossible to reach by telephone. Every time we called to ask for the promised materials, she was out of town, or in class, or at a meeting, and so we were forced to cultivate an intimate telephone relationship with her assistant, who tried valiantly to convey our messages and pin her down. Her speaking schedule was a nightmare, and she must have crossed the continent six times during the semester we were desperate to contact her.

Later, when I saw her teach at the retreat, I could see why everybody wanted Lee Knefelkamp; we wanted her too. But her procrastination and avoidance caused both of us a lot of angst. No one had time to read the materials, and besides that, I felt demeaned. I even thought it might have been a matter of hierarchy, that we were not important enough, or Touro was not a good enough law school, to merit her prompt attention. But when I met her, and saw how her whirlwind life was wearing on her body and her spirit, my anger subsided. I realized that she is just another woman who does not know how to say no, who commits herself to more contracts than any one person can perform. I had the feeling that she was not protecting her health, or her private life, or her sanity. She was actually quite fragile.

The retreat was held at the historic Three Village Inn in Stony Brook on two blustery days in early December. The Three Village Inn was built in 1751 and has retained its colonial quaintness. The walls are splashed with Laura Ashley's interpretation of the eighteenth century, and antiques abound; the staff members wear costumes of the era. Under my feet, the hardwood floors squeaked cheerfully, and through the glass windows, there was a wobbly version of the restless grey harbor and the silhouette of bare branches against a pewter sky. It was winter in Long Island when water, wind, and willows are better contemplated from the warm hearth inside.

And that is where the faculty and the members of the law school administration were gathered: around that warm hearth. The fire crackled, and we drank coffee and ate sticky cinnamon rolls, waiting for Lee Knefelkamp to arrive. A limousine had been dispatched to pick her up at Teachers College, and the fierce wind of an impending northeaster made the travel on the Northern State Parkway slow going. Finally she arrived at the Three Village Inn around ten o'clock, and once she thawed out, we started the retreat.

When a gifted individual begins to teach, there is often a change in the body brought about by a change in the spirit. Desire fuels the transformation. This past year, I watched two sets of videotapes featuring Joseph Campbell, one set a series of interviews by Bill Moyers, the other tapes of Campbell in the classroom. I have to confess that in the Moyers interviews, I never really understood what Joseph Campbell was talking about; for me, listening to him was like reading Heidegger, except that I substituted my confusion over *"Da-sein"* for confusion over "bliss." But in the videos in which Campbell was teaching, if bliss confused me, it did not matter. Even in reproduced form, I could witness the transformation in his body, the rhythms of his speech, the sweeping movements of his arms, the way he raised his eyebrows and gasped—barely audibly—right after he uttered a beautiful phrase. He was electrically charged when he was teaching. I saw desire work its way through his physical being as he tried to share with me why he found those myths so moving, so timeless, so deeply disturbing. He loved those stories and images so much that it became for him a matter of life and death to make me love them too. That is what teaching, and ultimately the perpetuation of culture, is all about: the transmission of desire. While I may still not understand bliss, I know where Joseph Campbell found his.

The same thing happened to Lee Knefelkamp at our retreat: she underwent a metamorphosis. Most of her presentation was a version of William Perry's scheme of cognitive development, and how it might apply to our lives as law teachers. She started the lecture out in that same curt, businesslike manner I had witnessed at our interview many months ago, but within half an hour she was a different being. Her face was lit up by some inner light. Her body, once reserved and stiff, became supple and quick, darting back and forth from the podium to the easel to write something down. She hummed when someone asked a question that she liked, as if she had been offered something delicious to eat. And the woman was wildly witty. Sometimes she laughed irrepressibly at her own funny comments, sometimes she did not, peering out at us over the top of her glasses to see if we had gotten the joke. Getting the joke was a sign that we were getting used to Perry's scheme—and to her.

I had read one of Perry's articles on cognitive development in preparation for the retreat, and found it both intriguing and baffling.[3] To have Knefelkamp distill the various stages of development in a student's patterns of thought from a daunting nine to a manageable four was helpful. But without Knefelkamp's endorsement of Perry's scheme—and that inner glow—I would not have cared. Whatever its significance, the ideas would have floated momentarily on the oily surface of my mind, and then slid off into the deep reservoir of articles read but promptly forgotten. In her presence I felt her passion for this subject, and somehow that passion was transferred to me. I will die with the Perry scheme embedded in my brain. What a magic trick.

Perry's insight is that each student operates out of an interpretive framework through which he gives meaning to his learning experience. The student's interpretive framework is not static; rather, it evolves as the student moves from one structure of meaning to another. This movement is sequential, and each stage includes and transcends the earlier positions. Perry refers to the development as a "Pilgrim's Progress," one marked by transitional stages as the student moves from a familiar, simpler pattern of meaning to a more complex reinterpretation of the world.[4] This scheme of development, or "map of sequential interpretations of meaning," has been found to be characteristic of students' cognitive and ethical development in a variety of educational environments, even—Knefelkamp promised us—in the law school.[5]

Knefelkamp's analysis of learner characteristics was based on a truncated version of Perry's scheme. The first Position in her scheme was "Dualism." A Dualistic thinker is one who believes that all knowledge is known, and that knowledge is nothing more than a collection of information, making for only one right answer to every question. Indeed, all meaning is divided into two realms: right or wrong, good or bad, success or failure, black or white. This view of knowledge leads the Dualistic thinker to perceive the role of the teacher as the transmitter of correct information, and the corresponding role of the student as its dutiful receiver. As Perry puts it, "Knowledge and goodness are perceived as quantitative accretions of discrete rightness to be collected by hard work and obedience."[6]

The way I understand it, the law student who argues that

he deserves a high grade because of how hard he studied, not to mention the length of his multivolume outline of the course, is a Dualist. Under Dualism, authority is "perceived as grading on amount of rightness, achieved by honest hard work, and as adding an occasional bonus for neatness and 'good expression.' "[7] When the old morality of reward for diligence crumbles, the student becomes disillusioned. Perry quotes the following familiar sad story from one of his students: "A lot of people noticed this throughout the year, that the mark isn't proportional to the work. 'Cause on a previous paper I'd done a lot of work and gotten the same mark, and on this one I wasn't expecting it. . . . In prep school it was more of a, more, the relationship was more personal and the teacher could tell whether you were working hard, and he would give you breaks if he knew you were working.' "[8] Hence the Dualist's offering of his five-pound outline of the course: proof of diligence, and diligence deserves reward.

In law school, another way to detect a Dualist is by checking his locker for commercial outlines. Commercial outlines are condensations of black letter law, and many first-year law students believe that academic success will be achieved by memorizing every rule in them. Before I knew anything about the Perry scheme, or what Dualism was, I used to label those students early medievalists—students of Augustine. In the early fifth century, Augustine wrote that intellectual training had only one purpose: to enhance an understanding of the Bible. Intellectual curiosity and originality were to be shunned. The emphasis was on amassing a body of knowledge that consisted of sets of rigid rules. Like other Dualists, Augustine had the utmost respect for authority, and "believed in dragons because they had been described in books."[9] His pedagogy was consistent with his Dualistic tendencies. In his book on teaching, *On Catechizing the Unlearned,* Augustine advocated that the rudiments of Christian doctrine be presented in a simple fashion, orally, and that the teacher "was to avoid excessively lengthy presentations and speak in a simple, thoroughly comprehensible manner."[10] The best books for the enterprise were called "handbooks," in which all the Christian doctrine was condensed for the student to memorize. Many students who come to law school in the late twentieth century believe that Augustine's theory of education should still prevail. And if a commercial outline described him, those same students would believe in a gigantic scaly-skinned reptile, with the claws of a lion, the tail of a serpent, and a glorious set of wings.

Both Knefelkamp and Perry seemed optimistic about how few Dualists—or students of Augustine, if you prefer—are actually running around the halls of academe. Perry writes, "no freshman still spoke from this Position in its purest form."[11] At the retreat, Knefelkamp too shrugged off the possibility that many Dualists could have made it as far as law school, but there was laughter in the audience. Many of us thought she was wrong—you and I, for example. So did Hazel Weiser, our good friend and colleague. After the retreat, Hazel shared one of her journals about her first-year law students with me, which I now share with you. She wrote:

This obsession with grades is distracting students from the more successful route of being motivated by their own curiosity and desire to discover the information and the strategies. This is so disappointing to me. One student kept on referring to her process which included asking herself constantly what I wanted from her. I told her that she should be asking herself how to solve the problem, not wasting her time second-guessing what I am looking for in any submissions. Clearly, students do not trust me or any other faculty at this time of year when they are obsessed with grades and disappointed that the amount of work was not commensurate with the grades they received.[12]

Hazel also wrote in her journal about another attribute of a Dualist. It is a theory of knowledge that I call "photocopamania." A photocopamaniac ascribes to the belief that one may acquire knowledge through the copying of texts. To copy the book is to know it. Photocopamania is consistent with Perry's idea that a Dualist regards knowledge as a quantitative accretion of "discrete rightness" that can be harvested by hard work in the fields. Hence the crazed photocopying; the quantitative accretion of paper becomes conflated with the quantitative accretion of knowledge. Similarly, a Dualist, or student of Augustine, would believe that he could keep others from doing well if he could keep the competitor from acquiring the mound of "discrete rightness," providing a motive for stealing books from the library. Again in her journal, Hazel wrote:

I received comments from the library staff about the conduct of students in the library. Although we are permitting collaboration, students are still secreting books and articles. They are also piling up around the computers, using them mainly to print out entire cases without even reading them. I wrote a memo to the first year class which addresses the librarian's complaints. I tried to explain that by printing out entire cases without reading them, students were actually increasing their stress levels. First, they were postponing the actual work on the project, and second, they were generating piles of work which looks far more formidable when approached in one pile rather than apprehended gradually. Their lack of discrimination is so debilitating. I am going to read more from the retreat's cherished notebook of cognitive theory materials to determine how I might inspire more mature attitudes towards complex tasks.[13]

Not only did you and I and Hazel think that Dualists abounded in the law school; we had our fair share of Early Multiplicitists as well. "Early Multiplicity" was the next position up the ladder of learning under the Perry scheme, as distilled by Lee Knefelkamp. An Early Multiplicitist recognizes the legitimacy of diverse opinions and values, at least in certain pockets of life where the right answers are not yet known. There is still a belief in a right answer for every question, but the state of our knowledge is incomplete; not all questions have been answered. In the meantime, we must be comfortable with multiple possible answers, and until certainty has been arrived at, all speculation stands on equal footing. The Early Multiplicist makes no distinction between legitimate abstract thought and what Perry calls "bull." [14]

The result of Early Multiplicity thinking can be unbridled relativism. In this domain of uncertainty, merely having an opinion makes it just as "right" as any other competing point of view. Perry characterizes this stage as a form of personalism: "The pure statement that, in the domain of uncertainty, to 'have' an opinion makes it as 'right' as any other expresses an egocentric personalism that we call multiplicity." [15] The egalitarian spirit of Early Multiplicity also diminishes respect for the teacher, and engenders cynicism about the teacher's assessment of student work. This is particularly true when the old standards of "rightness" and hard work have disappeared. The students at this stage feel bitterness when "they see the 'bullster' winning honors while they themselves work hard and receive C's." [16] There has been a loosening of the tie between authority and the guarantee of right answers; grading appears arbitrary and subjective.

Students who are upset about a poor grade often employ an Early Multiplicity argument to shrug it off. The assessment becomes personalized; the teacher's grade represents just one opinion in a vast sea of possible opinions, and therefore does not need to be taken seriously. This is particularly true when the recipient is a young man who is angry about receiving a poor grade from a woman teacher. It's bad enough to get a D, but to get a D from *her?* Hazel and our other colleagues in Legal Methods talk about this a lot, Deborah, confrontations over grades and lack of credibility with their students. The institution's low opinion of the Legal Methods faculty is never articulated, but is delivered tacitly by having their tiny offices located in a warren down by the soda machines. And all of the Legal Methods faculty are women, Deborah, which must send some message of inferiority. I have even heard other faculty members (all of them male) saying, in effect, that the Legal Methods teachers live in the basement apartments of life's high-rise. No wonder Legal Methods faculty complain so much about grade challenges. Under Early Multiplicity, the grade is personalized, identified with the giver, and not with the work being assessed. For an angry male student, it represents nothing more than her opinion, and let's face it, who is she?

I saw this combination of Early Multiplicity and sexist attitudes toward women faculty one day during judicial clerkship interviews. On the Judicial Clerkship Committee, we interview students, screen those for whom the committee will issue a letter of recommendation, and counsel all candidates on their writing samples, résumés, and so on. The constituency of the committee changes from time to time. We try to use our state and federal retired judges as interviewers, but we also have used various faculty members, preferably those with judicial clerkship experience. One year, during an afternoon of interviews, the committee consisted of myself, Deborah Bartel, who had served as a clerk for the Honorable James Hunter III of the Third Circuit, and Barbara Mehrman, the director of career planning. The three of us interviewed Number One in his class. (You know who he is, Deborah.) Number One is one of the most arrogant young men I have ever met. As far as I could tell, his rank in the class was just a ratification of his own worldview. He had always been Number One. He treated it as both his expectation and his due.

Sometimes I think an entire generation of parents overdid it with the manufacture of self-esteem, or perhaps they misunderstood the true nature of self-esteem. It is entirely acceptable to exclaim over your seven-year-old's literary efforts and treasure them for the rare manuscripts they are. But I think somewhere along the road to maturity, it is equally acceptable to say gently to your child, this work product is not your best; I know it would be if you only put more effort into it and understood the task. Try again. Unfortunately, I am certain that Number One's mother never offered constructive criticism or contemplated the idea that it was necessary. As he grew into his adult teeth and face, she continued to ooh and ah over his every breath, his every utterance, his every literary effort, and her unrelenting, unconditional praise and adulation created a monster. He was insufferable, and in my mind, had not one ounce of genuine self-esteem. Self-esteem comes from knowing you can do the job because you have done other jobs before, and most of the time, with a lot of hard work and a little luck, things have turned out all right. Self-esteem does not come from knowing you can do the job because your mother thinks you are the Buddha.

As is frequently the case, Number One in his law school class had a weak writing sample. Often the Judicial Clerkship Committee interviews are uncomfortable because we are casting a critical eye on the work of students who are at the top of their classes—talented, diligent students who are accustomed to academic success. Most of them are mature about taking criticism and advice, but some are not. As you can imagine, Deborah, Number One was one of the latter. I expressed concern that his writing sample was not good enough to submit to a federal judge, and he was not gracious. His first response was that he had gotten an A on the paper, so "someone must have thought it was pretty good." (Translation: someone male, someone with authority. I could not tell him the truth: the professor who had given him the A had a reputation for barely skimming his students' papers.) Undaunted, and piqued, Deborah Bartel proceeded to demonstrate why his paragraphing was poor, his diction imprecise, and his syntax convoluted, to which he responded, "Well, that's just your opinion. Others have read this paper and deemed it excellent. And in my opinion, it's excellent as well." Deborah handed him back his paper and said, "Well, Mr. X, that may be your opinion, but your opinion is just wrong." Then she turned to me and said, "I believe we are ready for the next interview." Taking her cue, I stood up and ushered the startled Number One to the door. After he was gone, we ranted and raved for a while, and then issued the usual letter to students who are at the top of their class but have weak writing samples: the committee will issue a letter of recommendation when Number One presents a stronger writing sample. He never did.

Eventually the learner leaves the stage of Early Multiplicity and lurches into what Knefelkamp called "Late Multiplicity." A Late Multiplicitist leaves the world of "right" and "wrong" answers, and comes to accept the notion of a "better" answer. An individual must now accept responsibility for an opinion: facts or text presented in its support; assumptions expressed and owned up to; a logical sequence of thoughts toward a conclusion—whatever criteria prevail in that particular discipline. There is a renewed respect for the teacher, not as a provider of right answers but as a guide for a new way of thinking.[17] Each sphere of human endeavor has its own patterns of thought, its own hierarchy of authority, and its own notions of a "better" answer. The Late Multiplicitist looks to the teacher to illuminate him about that "better answer," what standards it is judged by, and how it is arrived at. Cynicism about grading also disappears because what is being assessed is no longer the destination, but how the student got there.

The last position in these learning schemes Knefelkamp called "Contextual Relativism"; Perry called it "Commitment." Here is the way it is supposed to work: the learner is eventually required to make choices among equally good alternatives. These choices might be of values, politics, career paths, or personal relationships, and they are made affirmatively, even in the face of diverse, responsibly arrived at opinions. It is at this stage that the student experiences true agency; these commitments are the student's, and his alone, and it is his life that will be shaped and ordered by them.

The student may suffer emotional turmoil as he moves from Early Multiplicity to Commitment. Establishing priorities "can lead to periodic experiences of serenity and well-being in the midst of complexity."[18] The student fluctuates between order and disorder, and in "the loneliness or separateness implicit in these integrations and reintegrations, students seek among their elders for models . . . not only of knowledgability but of courage to affirm commitment in full awareness of uncertainty."[19]

As we have talked about many times, Deborah, I have trouble writing and thinking about this fourth and final stage, Commitment. It is difficult for me to articulate what my own commitment is, probably because I have not yet achieved it, or if I have, I don't recognize what it might be. This discomfort with Commitment may stem from having lived so much of my adult life in a law school. Roger Cramton explains: "The law teacher typically avoids explicit discussion of values in order to avoid 'preaching' or 'indoctrination.' His value position or commitment is not thought to be relevant to class discussion; students are left to decipher his views from the verbal and non-verbal cues that he provides."[20]

Furthermore, Cramton argues, a pedagogy that devotes more time to law application than to law creation will foster an environment in which questions of commitment rarely come up: "[V]alues are much more easily taken for granted in law application contexts than in law creation, since the lawyer involved in establishing a private or public regime of law from scratch must evaluate and refine values as part of this task. In creating a legal regime, the lawyer cannot take values for granted; they must be explicitly identified if the lawyer is to know what he creates."[21]

I would like to hide behind Roger Cramton's excuses for my lack of commitment, or failure to recognize it. I suspect, however, that the reasons are far more complex. Blaming my lack of commitment on the norms of classroom discussion or styles of pedagogy is like trying to stir a can of paint with a toothpick. I also find the notion that I am supposed to provide a student with emotional support as he fluctuates from order to disorder alarming. It implies that I have myself arrived safely at some kind of order, my own version of Commitment, and we both know, Deborah, that is untrue. I fluctuate all the time, but from a state of moderate disorder to one of utter chaos. My sense of humor is the only thing that keeps me on track—and my discipline. Students are free to witness and appropriate my survival techniques, but I cannot help them learn to swim when I can't keep my own head above water.

Even though I have great respect for Perry and Knefelkamp, there is a smugness about their theories that bothers me—an unspoken premise that these metateachers, these teachers of teachers, have themselves reached pedagogical nirvana. The model has the teacher at stage 4, or 9—whatever represents the highest mountain peak—with the students down below in altitude, scrambling up the scree. In the afternoon session of the retreat, after our loud and too long lunch, the questions asked of and by Lee Knefelkamp were all about how the teacher in the upper stratosphere could reach those goats who were down below. But what happens when the teacher turns out to be a horned, bearded, ruminant animal herself? It is so hard to hold a piece of chalk with a cloven hoof.

When I first read Perry's work, and later when I watched Lee Knefelkamp draw her scheme on a smooth white surface with a squeaky black marker that smelled of summer camp labels, I found myself looking furtively for myself. Where did I fit into the scheme? On what rung of the ladder of learning was I stuck? What if she gets to stage 2, and that is all of her theory I can understand? Or what if she describes all the stages and I understand them all, but discover that I am drifting somewhere between 3 and 4? What good will I derive from all of this cognitive theory if my own stage of intellectual development turns out to be a bonsai in a bowl and not a California Redwood?

After she finished with Perry's scheme, Lee Knefelkamp had some more practical advice. She suggested that at the beginning of our courses, we make an evaluation of the level of cognitive development of each student in the class. While there wasn't time for her to go into the methods of evaluation, it was clear that someone knowledgeable had developed diagnostic tests to locate an individual at his appropriate level: 1, 2, 3, or 4. I felt certain I lacked the competence to administer such a test. Besides, in a class of almost ninety students, it would be administratively impossible for me to do this. I have enough trouble learning all their names, let alone the status of their cognitive development.

I also rejected the idea for more substantive reasons. I was afraid that by classifying my students at one level or another, the classification would color my perception of them, individually or as a group. In my readings about education, I ran into an educator, Peter McLaren, who had observed that labels imposed by teachers on certain classes of students reinforced stereotypes and resulted in programs that denied equal opportunities. In the Catholic school in Toronto that McLaren studied, there was a system of classification that ranked students according to academic standing, resulting in what McLaren called "reification" or the objectification of students. McLaren wrote, "The instructional rituals were linked to reification in a number of contexts. For instance, from the teacher's perspective, students were looked upon as 'level threes and fours.' Many of them were described as 'rude' and 'bad-mannered.' . . . Collectively they were described as 'low' or 'basic level' group. . . . One of the consequences of this reification was that 'basic level' programmes were created to fit an instructional paradigm for the 'below average' student. This further reinforced the perception that immigrant students were 'dysfunctional.' "[22]

I did not want this to happen. I did not want to pass a student in the hall, say hello and silently utter to myself, "Aha, there goes a Dualist, stuck in a rut, stuck in the mud, stuck at level 2 forever." I don't even look at the grades I give my students, so that I can continue to think of them as human beings with only a name attached to them, not an A or a C. After grading final exams, I turn in to the registrar a set of grades for a set of numbers and I never connect up the names and faces to the grades they receive in Property. With respect to their grades, I find great relief in their anonymity.

Even though I didn't want to locate my students on the cognitive development spectrum, there was another part of

Knefelkamp's advice that struck me as good, and concrete. She recommended that we sit down with our assigned materials and list what kinds of intellectual tasks the course required and how we intended to assess success. She even made the radical suggestion that we design our exams to test whether the students have indeed mastered the tasks that we have chosen for them to tackle. Then she urged us to communicate this information to our students. From the vantage point of someone taking notes at the retreat, this advice looked easy enough to follow, and I pledged to give it a try in my Property class next semester. I was looking for some concrete, discrete experiment—something I could actually accomplish within the context of my harried life.

I know it drove you nuts, Deborah, that I was willing to wade right in without having mapped out the terrain hidden beneath the water. You wanted to read absolutely everything about cognitive theory before you were willing to commit yourself to an experiment in the classroom. I was willing to just read selectively and to digest that Perry article over and over again, and then launch a small project and try it out. My methodology had nothing to do with how I think such a project ought to be undertaken. Ideally, your way seems the right way, to read broadly and deeply, but it took you over a year to digest that material, Deborah, and I didn't have that long. My dissertation cast its shadow over every step I took last year; indeed, it still casts its shadow over every step I take. What will life be like when I can once again feel the sun on my back?

Also, Deborah, there is that other very real fact about my

life: I have three small children. What can I say about Nan, Kate, and Johanna? I would never say they cast a shadow over every step I take; indeed, whatever sunlight I get is reflected off their funny faces. I am lucky that Dan does a lot of child care, but even he would admit that the maintenance of the house, the food preparation, the dirty clothes, the bathing, the books at night, the doctors' appointments, the homework, the ferrying from place to place—the bulk of it falls on me. I don't mean to complain. My girls were not unwanted children who cut short a brilliant career; they were wonderful late-life surprises who arrived in the middle of an erratic one. You know they are lovely, Deborah, from our frequent forays to the playground or to the beach. But the girls are also a tremendous responsibility, and sometimes, to give them the attention they deserve, I do not—cannot—do things the right way. And so I settle for less, and try to do things the best way I can under the circumstances.

I cannot tell you how I envied those many nights when you worked and worked and worked at school, for long stretches at a time, how I envied all those books you read for this project, how I envied you Christopher, your own source of light—an independent adolescent who was secretly hoping that you might work late. Your life looks so whole to me, and my life so sliced into thin little pieces; my writing too. That's just the way it has to be, though, Deborah, for the time being. What looks like a choice—to read an article deeply, to meditate on it for months on end—is indeed a choice, but not about the proper methodology. It is a choice about setting priorities, about joy, and what matters to me. It might even be a commitment.

Well, Deborah, I have done my work in the garden; I have described the form and substance of the retreat, and have at least taken a stab at presenting Perry's scheme of cognitive development. You take over now, since you planted most of the seeds for the second day of the retreat.

I am going to finish this season with my memories of that night. It is a rare occurrence indeed, to spend twenty-four hours with your colleagues; the night was more like a slumber party. We broke up into little groups, not along predictable political cleavages, but along the superficial cracks of inclination. Some of us cruised the outlet stores near the inn, bonding in an orgy of gratuitous spending. Others braved the wind and walked down by the harbor. A few took naps; a few curled up by the fire and drank. That night we had a raucous dinner and roasted our departing colleague, Dinesh Khosla, who was returning to CUNY Law School, leaving a void in our academic family.

And then, just as if the Retreat Committee had planned it, there was a total lunar eclipse. It was a particularly splendid casting of the sun's shadow because of recent volcanic eruptions in the Philippines, Chile, and Alaska. Usually total lunar eclipses transform the moon to a dark red disc; the only sunlight that hits the moon is filtered through and refracted by the earth's atmosphere. This eclipse was different; the airborne ash and dust blocked most of the sunlight, and the moon became an ominous black smudge. A few of us stood together in silence, drunk on wine and the fragrance of Crabtree and Evelyn, and watched as a giant thumb put out the silver light.

53

FOUR

Summer

THE
SECOND
DAY
OF THE
RETREAT

As we originally conceived of this project, Louise, it had a nice feel to it, a certain simplicity, a certain neatness. We had compartmentalized the activities: reading, listening, doing. Yet there was a complexity, a layered feeling to the process we envisioned. With the help of a second consultant, William M. Welty, we would teach ourselves how to teach others.[1] Our examination of the way we learn, our participation in a learning activity, would provide us with the skills to teach others and insight into the learning process.

We had laid out the tools and the seeds: the reading and Lee Knefelkamp's lecture. Now, on the second day, we were supposed to get our hands dirty. We were all supposed to muck around with ideas. This is praxis, isn't it, the part where we plant the seeds or the bulbs and wait to see what germinates?[2] We assumed our colleagues knew how to use a trowel, so we could move on to the more important issues. We wanted to sit down with them and discuss the way our garden should grow. We wanted to discuss the possibilities of a late planting, color and texture, size and shape; we wanted to talk about our vision, our collective imaginings of the profusion of color we hoped for in late summer or early fall. The problem was that the trowels and the seeds seemed to have been left behind, and no one wanted to talk about the way the garden should look.

I don't think of this as our failure. It is just that our expectations were too high. And if I was disappointed with the second day of the retreat, perhaps it was because I saw things "through a glass darkly,"[3] dimmer and murkier than they might have been otherwise. My experience of that day, of the people and the events, is tangled up with events occurring three thousand miles away in a suburb of San Diego where Cheryl, my best friend, was dying.

Carole, Cheryl's sister, called me a couple of days before. It is happening too quickly, she said. You need to come right away.

I convinced myself that it wouldn't be right to leave you and Peter. But in some other part of my heart, I knew that the reason I didn't book an immediate flight to California was a wish on my part to avoid the deathwatch. You introduced me, and legal literature, to the deathwatch the summer before. The beautiful and melancholy language you used to describe this unavoidable human ritual did not make me long to participate in such an event.[4] I wanted to believe that I had already said my good-byes sitting at Cheryl's side in the cool, dim recesses of a hospital emergency room, where we escaped the demands of children and the expectations she had for her last summer in Maine, and waited for word that it wasn't time yet.

It wasn't time yet, but we both knew that the time was close at hand. At the end of the summer, the day Chris and I drove away from the apartment we had shared with Cheryl, her two sons, and various and assorted friends and family members for nine summers, Cheryl extracted a promise from me: I'll see you at Christmas, she repeated firmly, not once but twice.

It was too early, two weeks before Christmas, when the call came. We don't know how much longer she has. Come quickly. She is dying.

What I saw and heard at the retreat is colored by a sense of loss and a preoccupation with responsibility—the duty of one woman friend to another, the duty of colleagues to one another and to the students they teach. What we are able to see is affected by so many other contingencies. My contingency that winter night was death, approaching as steadily as the nor'easter, a rare winter hurricane that arrived late in the afternoon the second day of the retreat, leveling trees, destroying beach homes, and causing planes to crash in less time than it took for me to get from the Three Village Inn to a local airport.

It was fairly easy to cruise through the retreat in spite of personal distractions. The whole thing was on autopilot except for menu selections. It was all planned in advance, and the responsibility for leading us through the process was delegated to experts like Lee Knefelkamp and William Welty. We had selected three problems for discussion in small working groups which would then report back to the whole faculty. The first problem was supplied by William Welty and adapted for the law school setting by Peter Zablotsky. Peter, who was tenure track then and is tenured now, began his career as a playwright and a member of the Legal Methods faculty. In the problem constructed by Peter, a student of color is failed by a white woman faculty member, a fictional Edwina Armstrong, who decides that the student has a writing problem. In the law school setting, the woman faculty member becomes a member of the Legal Methods faculty. Our Legal Methods faculty is immediately on the defensive.

We have seen two men and one woman make the transition from non–tenure-track legal methods courses—introductory courses in legal research and writing—to tenure-track or "substantive" courses. Peter was the last. The dean recently gave notice. A barrier had gone up with little explanation. Suddenly there was a line that could not be crossed. The rights of full participation in the community, including the right to vote, lay on one side of that line. Approximately 50 percent of the women on the faculty were on the other side. Any "rights" the Legal Methods faculty have exist at the sufferance of the tenured faculty. It takes a two-thirds vote to give them the right to vote at faculty meetings.

The hypothetical intervention by the administration because of allegations by the student of racism and bias did not raise issues about cognitive theory, learning styles, or the position of the student within the developmental framework described by Lee Knefelkamp. I began to wonder whether anyone else heard Lee Knefelkamp say something about the position of women and students of color in the Perry scheme. Late in the afternoon, just before she left, she mentioned that women and students of color begin beyond Dualism, at a place in her model where both the contestability of knowledge and the way it is interconnected begin to be appreciated. If women and students of color are "advanced" within this scheme, why are they often "behind" when their exams are graded? This was the question I wanted to address. But we were mired in the kind of discussion you would expect in a hierarchical system where responsibility for teaching writing skills is transferred to a specialized, untenured, exclusively female faculty.

It is always disturbing when you find yourself publicly disagreeing with or challenging the assertions of a colleague who is in a vulnerable place. I didn't want to quarrel with the Legal Methods faculty, now all women, who bear the brunt of the worst gender bias in our institution. But on the issue of race and the propriety of intervention by the administration to deal with allegations of racism, some members of the Legal Methods faculty speak in the kind of absolutes that place us on opposite sides of a huge divide.

The problem about the Black student raises an issue of aesthetics, of the teacher's preference for a particular writing style. I think we should talk about the relationship between rules and aesthetics. Would anyone on this faculty recognize certain usages as cultural? I mention Zora Neale Hurston and her attempt to describe the way Black people use English.[5] Would any of my colleagues recognize the transformation of a noun into a verb as a cultural phenomenon? I once had an older Black student complain in an essay that whites "majestify" themselves at the expense of Blacks. I chuckled when I read it and wrote him a note telling him that the word was just perfect for the essay that he was writing for me, but it might not fit within the context of formal legal writing. But why shouldn't he use it, or rather, why shouldn't I encourage him to use it? It is, after all, a challenge to the same hegemony that conceives of the Legal Methods faculty as inferior.

Even before I finish speaking and wait for the question to be reframed in a way that will preclude any discussion of possible cultural differences, I know that what I said was not heard. The women in Legal Methods want to talk about the really important work they do, the responsibility that has been placed on them and the impossibility of the task. And that means we have to talk about race another way, the old familiar way. Discussions of race have a pattern to them, assertions and challenges to those assertions, and I know my part. I have only to wait for my cue, to listen while one of the women who feels vulnerable defends her judgment and her power, using paternalism to feint and then deliver a stunning blow. Her credibility in question, she raises the specter of Black inferiority. This is, after all, a case where a Black woman student has been assigned to a "remedial" writing course. We are doing a disservice to our minority students, she says, when we admit them only to watch them fail. They are not equipped to handle law school because they cannot write.

There is my cue. Illiteracy is not a race issue, I chide my colleagues, except to the extent that there is a presumption that Black students are less qualified than their white counterparts. As all of us who make our students write know, many white students are poor writers. Big firms establish writing programs for incoming associates, and we all know those associates are not students of color. They are not our students. They are students from the schools way up the hierarchy of schools, schools catering to the "cognitive elite." I repeat my story about a classmate at Harvard, a white male, who was my partner for a project that required a written report. He could not write at all. When he felt my exasperation reading his paper, he defended himself with an assertion of superiority, a perfect score on the LSAT examination. In fact, I add, some of those who score highest on the LSAT are the ones who can't string two sentences together without borrowing those sentences from someone else.

Everything I've said is true. And yet I know how it sounds. Hyperbole countered with hyperbole—that is what is expected in discussions of race these days.

After lunch, we discussed two other problems. These problems were "law teaching dilemmas," essays written by the two of us, Louise. The essays didn't give the faculty the luxury or the mental distance that comes with pretending to solve some other person's problems. These were our problems, problems that occur in our institution and that our colleagues recognized immediately as their own.

Louise, you asked eloquently and simply about the problem of mistakes. When should a faculty member admit that he doesn't have the answer to a question or that he made a mistake about something he said in class? Yesterday, Perry, through his agent Lee Knefelkamp, attacked the idea that the teacher is the "giver" and the student the "receiver" of information, and yet today, when we grapple with the issue of our own vulnerability, we cling to the model that was criticized and labeled Dualism.[6]

While we don't deal with cognitive theory or Perry's model, we all agree there is an ethical issue here. You and I define the ethical issue in terms of honesty. While there are some among our male colleagues who agree with us, no women join the men who are resolute in their intention to maintain their own credibility, even at the expense of honesty. For these male colleagues, the ethical issue is the failure of the teacher to provide the correct information. And, in fact, this is the principal thrust of the conversation. All sorts of suggestions are made about the way a teacher can remedy an error, assuming that the lack of knowledge is an error or even (the worst-case scenario) that we got the facts or the law wrong.

These suggestions all implicate some position on the Perry intellectual continuum. The alternatives offered by our colleagues all involve strategies designed to avoid an admission of fallibility. How do we avoid giving an answer when we don't know what is right? One solution, sending the student out to research the problem, corresponds with the interpretation of a student located at Position 2: "Good Authorities give us problems so that we can learn to find the Right Answer by our own independent thought." [7] What do we do about making mistakes? The suggestion that we explain to the class that the problem had more complexity to it than we originally thought and that on reflection we decided there might be another answer, probably corresponds with Position 5: "Theories are not truths but metaphors to interpret data with. You have to think about your thinking."

Perry's scheme focuses on the meaning that is assigned to the learning experience by the student. The student is interpreting his or her task, but this interpretation does not take place in isolation. The student's interpretation refers to some communication that occurs in the classroom. The varied and contradictory perceptions students have of teachers may well have their source in the varied and contradictory perceptions teachers have of their role and the roles of their students.

We could turn Perry on his head—and perhaps we should—and look at the meaning the faculty assigns to the learning process. Do students ignore the meanings assigned by the faculty? If we adopt Perry's scheme as a means of positioning our colleagues along this continuum of possible meanings, some of them appear to be lumped around the end of the scale—stuck in Dualism. The faculty member at Position 2 feels compelled to fulfill the expectation of the student who says, "Authorities know, and if we work hard, read every word and learn Right answers, all will be well." That raises some interesting issues. What happens when a student has moved beyond the meaning assigned by the teacher? What answer to this dilemma would move us beyond Perry's Relativism? I think it might require honesty and an admission of fallibility, but that would mean surrendering the right to think of ourselves as Authorities with a capital A.

My law teaching dilemma discussed the frustration I feel trying to reach 106 students in a way which engages all of them. I know I am failing. I can feel them falling through the cracks. I can sense their lack of comprehension, but their posture and studiously blank faces plead with me to leave them in peace.

I wrote down my ideas about the reasons we fail—the size and configuration of the room, the acoustics, the futility of attempts at class participation, the inattentiveness of students who are burnt out after their first year, or so driven in their second and third years to improve their résumés that they overextend themselves as law clerks or student leaders. In its original form, my problem was rejected by the Retreat Committee. I was told there were too many issues in this problem. It would distract and confuse our colleagues. William Welty assumed responsibility for making it more manageable.

I suppose my dilemma could have stimulated discussion about the differences in the meaning assigned by students and faculty to the classroom experience. Instead, we spent significant amounts of time discussing the troublemakers and the ne'er-do-wells, the lack of real commitment and discipline on the part of our students. We could have explored Perry's concept of Commitment, or more precisely, multiple, competing Commitments. Perry understands that energy, action, and time are not inexhaustible. Multiple Commitments require judgments about priorities.[8] We could have discussed how we feel about the judgments our students make and how or why we go about challenging those judgments. Instead, I found myself marveling at an orgy of student bashing, a serious discussion of the various tactics that could be used to shame or coerce students into preparing for class.

It's funny, really. There we were, a group of people who hadn't read the assignment, who spent last night reveling and short-sheeting beds as though this were summer camp rather than an academic retreat. A bunch of noisy siblings who wouldn't settle down and go to sleep—that's what it sounded like the night before. I didn't join in the games (I'd begged off because I was ill), but I know that the silliness and playfulness of my colleagues are what allow us to live together; they are the source of the affection that overrides some very painful political disagreements. Still, it did seem ludicrous in the morning to sit there while we postured and harrumphed and spoke righteously about the need to instill self-discipline in our students.

The dilemma employs evening students to highlight the problems of juggling multiple commitments. Some of our students are older than we are. They work an eight- or ten-hour day and then commute an hour or more each way to attend law school. The discussion proceeds as though this were irrelevant. These are the times when I wish the connections, the contingencies that affect our lives, were visible—like the symptoms of my cold.

I once got into a wrangle with a colleague about the grades he gave out one semester. He failed over one-third of his class. He insisted that his test was objective and that they deserved to fail. I thought his mother's death and his own illness that semester had left him vulnerable to a perceptual disorder, like someone who has been transported into an alternative universe in which everything is upside down and wrong side round. Asking him to see the relationship between his emotional distress, his mother's death, his own illness, and his evaluation of the answers students gave to exam questions was like asking for a miracle. You might as well be Bernadette at Lourdes, asking Mary to prove she's really there.

The allusion is not accidental. Whenever I have a conversation about perception, about racism or sexism or the conditional nature of reality, particularly when it is a conversation with a male colleague, I feel like a mystic among a crowd of empiricists and skeptical rationalists. What I am trying to describe, from a metaphysical point of view, is less like the Lady of Lourdes and more like a distortion in the space/time continuum, a favorite among science fiction writers. You can see a wormhole or a wrinkle in time when you are in hyperspace, or in the reality we create with our imagination. But there is nothing to make contingencies and coincidences of everyday life visible to those whose lack of imagination pins them to the earth.

The retreat ended as the Nor'easter arrived, compounding my guilt and delaying my trip to California one more day.

After the session ended, William Welty offered his condolences. "I am afraid we did not do justice to your problem," he said.

Fall

BEFORE
THE
FROST

FIVE

Fall

BRINGING
IN THE
HARVEST:
PERRY,
PROPERTY,
AND
THE LOST
SEASON

The idea, Deborah, was for us to take the insights of Knefel-kamp and Perry and put them to use in our teaching. I chose my Property class. As you know, Property has always weighed heavily on me. I have never really known how or why to teach it. Rarely do I worry about my mission or how to accomplish it in Legal History or Jurisprudence. Those courses seem to teach themselves. A passion for history and ideas makes it easy, and sharing that passion has always been enough for me.

But Property is a different matter. As a teacher of a first-year course, I am forced upon the students; they have not chosen to be in the room with me. And with four credits, it is a lot of teaching, with much of the material like Hungarian food, dense and opaque, hard to pronounce and even harder to digest: estates in land, future interests, the rule against perpetuities, concurrent ownership, and for dessert, landlord/tenant law, steeped in apricot brandy.

The most painful aspect of Property is its unignorability. It is an important area of substantive law, one our students need to master not only to pass the bar exam, but also to be competent practitioners. In Property, I cannot be casual about coverage. I am not free to serve only dessert, even if dessert consists of palascintas, those lovely limp little pancakes, smothered in raisins and hot cream.

There are also too many students in Property, approximately ninety. I usually struggle to learn all their names from the seating chart, but success varies. Most semesters, I make an effort to wander into the cafeteria before class, to have coffee, to stop and chat at the tables, to greet my students informally. There we meet as equals, leveled by our need for caffeine. And some students themselves take the initiative to make themselves known to me, by showing up at office hours or by dogged class participation.

Most of the time, I really want to make contact with my students, but if I am in a writing blur, my interest in them as people lapses. I am ashamed to admit there have been semesters during which I have known only a handful of my

Property students' names. When I construct my personal history, I can gauge prior periods of preoccupation by the number of students whose names I cannot whisper as they walk across the stage at graduation. They are smiling faces that I recognize, but smiling faces with no identity.

From my law school days at Texas, with classes numbering 125, I remember the other side of too many students in Property. At least in my first year, I never knew my teachers; certainly there was no effort on their part to know me. There was one exception: my Civil Procedure teacher, George Schatzki. He had a tradition of inviting twenty students from the section he taught to his home on Sunday afternoons during the fall semester for tea. I went on my allotted day in the alphabet, and it was wonderful to see his wife and his cat, and to know that the top of his desk looked worse than mine. I still did not get to talk to the professor, but I so appreciated the gesture, to be invited into his home like a real person. Here was a law teacher who, in his own civilized way, was rebelling against too many students in his classroom—against the pernicious influence of anonymity—all with a cup of tea and Pepperidge Farm cookies, and what I now know to be a precious commodity, his time.

I wish more law teachers cared about getting to know their students. Do you remember, Deborah, last year when I was obsessing on law school architecture for a project that never came to fruition? I stumbled across this priceless quote from an article about the design of the eleven-story law school building at Chicago-Kent: "The faculty's desire to increase faculty/student contact led to the creation of floor-to-ceiling glass walls to link the perimeter office corridors to the library."[1] What kind of increased faculty/student contact do you think they envisioned? It sounds like an aquarium, an academic Sea World, where one set of mammals pays money to look through a giant glass wall at another set of mammals—except that dolphins are more appealing than most law professors.

The architectural solution at Chicago-Kent reveals the contours of the real problem—the problem that was not articulated in the glossy pages of the magazine. Ideas, beliefs, and desires work their way through the buildings we design. The cement mixer is dumb; it does not churn with intent. But the pourer of that elephant-grey lava has been given a plan, a blueprint, and that blueprint has ideological content. It represents not only a vision of how the building should look, but a vision of how the world should look. By carving up space in a designated way and allocating usage to different classes of human beings, a blueprint communicates who is valued and who is not. It defines the community, and there are hidden messages in walls that separate, in the assignment of corner offices with a view, in the faculty elevator at the University of Texas that will not tolerate the weight of a student. My guess is that some committee of faculty members at Chicago-Kent must have said to their architect, "We need a wall that doesn't look like a wall. We want to keep the barrier, but create the illusion of access. We are willing to yield opacity."

The anonymity of students is not just a function of numbers; it is a state of mind. So it isn't just that there are too many students in Property. I have almost as many in

Jurisprudence, and the numbers there do not oppress me. You must feel it too, Deborah, when you teach Contracts in the second semester of a student's first year. What really adds emotional poundage to Property is its four-creditness, and its timing in the journey of the vulnerable student toward academic dismissal. A four-credit D or F at the end of the first year can easily cause a student to flunk out of law school.

I find it a melancholy task, reading and rereading the inevitable handful of unsatisfactory blue books, wondering if my assessment is going to shut the door forever on someone's entry into the legal profession. After a few days of agonizing, and asking myself over and over again, "Could I send an unsuspecting member of the public to this person with a legal problem involving real property?" I release the grades to the registrar, and set those few Ds and Fs out to sail.

Because of anonymous grading, I do not know to whom those grades belong, but it never takes long for their owners to come back to shore. I hear them first from shallow seas, on voice mail, those plaintive songs of embraced failure: "Professor Harmon, my name is———[the revelation], and I need to talk to you about my grade in Property." Almost always that revelation brings sorrow. It is a very particular sorrow, a teacher's sorrow, a discrete kind of soul wound, a paper cut that carves a thin, imperceptible line of blood into the skin. When they come to see me to discuss the exam, and we sit down face to face, I am overwhelmed by a sadness that sings not so much of, "Why did you fail?" but more of, "How did I fail you?"

Of course, I know that students fail for reasons other than bad teaching. Their lives fall apart; they are gripped by illness, or collide with a car. Sometimes they just don't study. But more often, I find myself sitting across the table from a hardworking, intelligent person who did not understand what the task was. That failure is shared property: it belongs to the student and it belongs to me.

It is difficult to characterize the nature of that shared property. It certainly was not a donative transfer. In no way did I "give" the D or the F to the student, although that is usually the student's metaphor of choice. Neither is it a form of concurrent ownership, since nominally the failure belongs to the student and not to me. Perhaps it is a simple trust relationship: the student holds legal title to the bad grade, but I am its equitable owner. Perhaps I should just give up on the law of property altogether as a means of explaining our shared interest in the student's D or F. The dark, mysterious language of criminal law beckons, with bony fingers pointing to multiple wrongdoers, allocated culpability, spilled blood, and the lure of conspiracy.

Whatever the metaphor, I often find that this student with whom I share this failure is one of my favorites, possessing a curious, interested face. It is a face that I seek out from the front of the classroom whenever I depart from the safety of the syllabus. I love to dip in and out of centuries, and in and out of books and ideas—I do so to avoid pedagogical burnout. How else could I, a thinking person, spend a decade imparting the difference between two future interests without running the risk of neural loss? To avoid losing my mind, I choose to talk about the more interesting aspects of future interests (and yes, Deborah, there really are some). The difference between the two future interests is presented in the book, I rationalize, and there is probably some computer software that can do a better job than I can. And when I venture forth into uncharted territory, I often rely on this student who has done poorly on the exam to lean forward, nod his head, and give other signals that he is interested. It is not uncommon for this student to participate actively and insightfully in class discussions, to have demonstrated a shared passion for history and ideas. It is also not uncommon for this student to be marginal—an older student, a person of color, a mother of three—someone who has traveled to law school over narrow, difficult byroads, and not the interstate.

During the ritual of "going over the exam," I almost always discover that the student has not demonstrated doctrinal competence. Rules, definitions, technical distinctions—the nuts and bolts of property law—are nowhere evident. And when I ask them about the gaps in the relevant law, they often have seemed genuinely surprised to learn that I wanted them filled in. In the past, I have found myself in a state of disbelief: how could they not know what I wanted them to know? But at the retreat, Lee Knefelkamp got me to thinking: how *could* they possibly know what I wanted them to know? Have I put them on notice that I demand doctrinal competence? Do they understand what doctrinal competence consists of?

Depending on the material, I may not even go over much doctrine in class. My assumption has always been that students are capable of achieving mastery over the relevant law without my assistance or intervention. My job is to facilitate the process of self-education: to choose a geographical destination, select a map, provide a historical perspective on the journey, bring color to those ancient words of property and undermine the starkness of their black and white. I have been less likely to dwell on the difference between a contingent remainder and a vested remainder subject to complete divestment than to explain the feudal worry over a gap in seisin, or to explore a twentieth-century analog to this dread.

But how and what I have taught in class is misleading; it is not a good gauge for what will be on the exam. Unfortunately this marginal student often does not perceive my unarticulated expectation of doctrinal competence. The failed exam may have more than its share of insightful, even inspired observations that have garnered praise in the classroom, but go unrewarded in a blue book. There may be an intelligent discussion of fourteenth-century real actions, but no real effort to distinguish among the future interests. And it is the latter that gets the points.

I have looked in the literature on cognitive theory, but to no avail, for a description of this kind of schizophrenia: a teacher who talks about one set of ideas in class and tests for mastery of another on the exam. I am not unique; many law teachers suffer from a similar kind of schizophrenia, although the more traditional diagnosis is the "Socratic method." Indeed, with the adoption in the late nineteenth century of the Socratic method as the dominant style of pedagogy, we institutionalized a severance between the classroom discussion and what was expected on the exam.

I simply cannot avoid writing about Christopher Columbus Langdell, Deborah. I know that when we discussed an earlier version of this manuscript, we wondered if my lengthy footnotes about Langdell should come up into text. You dropped heavy hints about how "everybody does Langdell," and how you weren't sure "Langdell was really relevant," and I have thought about your comments quite a bit. I think you are right: everybody does Langdell. But everybody *should* do Langdell. There is almost no aspect of the law school that was not influenced by the ideas of Langdell, or more broadly, by the late-nineteenth-century domination of empiricism and the scientific method in American universities. My error in the earlier version was to bury so much of the material on Langdell in footnotes. As so often happens in first drafts, the important stuff was below the line.

Christopher Columbus Langdell gets the credit and the blame for such reforms in legal education as the three-year curriculum, entrance exams, formal exams at the end of each year's study, the professional law school teacher, and the infamous case method. Langdell viewed the study of law as a science, in which students were to distill from the cases the abstract principles of law. The law library was the laboratory of the law, and his famous casebook in Contracts contained nothing but reprinted appellate court decisions. Through a game of cat and mouse between the teacher and the student, the rules of logic would be brought to bear upon a court's decision, and the student would eventually discover the law, or more precisely, it would be revealed to him through rigorous analysis. This manner of classroom discussion was not designed to promote clarity; rather, through the meanness of the Socratic dialogue, it often promoted obfuscation and the diminution of dignity.

Not only did Langdell's Socratic method result in a chasm between what happened in class and what was on the exam, it also institutionalized this time-honored tradition of abusing students publicly. Consider the learning environment in the classroom of William Keener, a law professor in the 1890s who developed a version of Langdell's case method at Columbia:

> With his bulky and bearlike figure, his great red beard, and his piercing, almost predacious eyes, Keener's physical appearance was most impressive, and his personal manner in the classroom was brutally aggressive. He would assault a student with a rapid fire of searching, provocative questions that soon drove the unwary legal neophyte into a ridiculous and untenable position. He seemed determined to prove to each student called up for interrogation that he was completely unqualified to discuss intelligently any legal point. The students thought him almost sadistic in his ruthless disregard for their personal dignity.[2]

The writer of this history goes on to report that students went through a period of hatred and humiliation, followed by a deep determination to be thoroughly prepared, and eventually discovered that "with Keener the student had learned more than he had learned from any other teacher in the Law School."[3]

Nowhere in the account of Keener's pedagogy is there any mention of those students who may have left the study of law due to this brand of terrorism. Neither has anyone sought to measure the permanent emotional damage that may have been caused by Keener and others like him. Unfortunately, Keener's approach is still sanctioned by legal educators in the late twentieth century. Consider these words from an essay by C. A. Peairs, Jr.: "I consider it legitimate to ask a student whether he is offering his knowledge or his wisdom. . . . I must repeat that the sarcastic, the ill-mannered, even the ill-tempered teacher is not necessarily a bad teacher. The top-blowers I have mentioned above were all, I think, very good teachers. The proof of the process is in what remains after memory has failed."[4] What do you think Peairs meant, Deborah? Does he mean bad manners and ill temper, and possibly sadism, are justified if the student has somehow managed to learn the law? To be fair to Langdell, there is no indication that he himself had a "ruthless disregard" for his students. Indeed there is little evidence to suggest that he had any regard for his students at all:

> Langdell himself was not a born teacher. The course of his entire thought was too deliberate and ponderous; he relied too entirely upon intellectual process to reach all classes of students . . . as he grew

81

older, his eyesight failed, and he was forced to rely entirely on lectures for conveying instruction; and many students found even greater difficulty in making much of his courses.[5]

Langdell did not turn out to be much of a writer either, although what he wrote was revealing. I was amused to find that he had authored two volumes, one entitled *A Summary of the Law of Contracts* (1880) and the other *A Summary of Equity Pleading* (1883). Each book was like a treatise, a condensation of the black letter law that was going to be on the exam but was never discussed in class. In the preface to the 1880 volume, Langdell (I assume) writes, "The following pages were first published as a supplement to the second edition of the writer's collection of Cases on Contracts. It was for that purpose that they had been written, and there was then no thought of issuing them in separate form. It was soon found, however, that many persons who wanted the Summary did not care for the Cases."[6] The popularity of these summaries of law reflects Langdell's version of the schizophrenia that has become the hallmark of legal education: what the teacher does in class bears little relation to what will be on the exam. Langdell even invented the answer to the student's prayer: the commercial outline.

I have fallen heir to this schizophrenia, but not to Langdell's version of it. My students still need to buy a commercial outline, but not because I am engaging them in the Socratic method. I do not like the Socratic method. For one thing, I am lousy at it and do not always think that quickly on my feet. No, my weakness is for history. This week in Property we did a famous judicial decision, one of Sir Edward Coke's—Spencer's case—and I spent twenty minutes on why it is impossible from the decision to tell who won the case or what the holding was. It required the class to discuss what it means to have a theory of precedent, and the importance of recording and publishing judicial opinions in developing the rule of law. We talked about Coke for a little, and looked at his rakish face on the wall in B-2, and I longed to tell them about Coke's many battles with James I, and what else was going on in the sixteenth century with the royal courts, but I stopped short after glancing at my watch. I had only fifteen minutes to cover covenants running with the land.

Langdell would not have approved, Deborah. He was so wedded to the idea that the law was a separate science that he would not countenance any courses in the curriculum at Harvard Law School that reflected a broader view of the law. Jurisprudence, for example, was offered only sporadically, with no courses in the philosophy of law being offered from 1883 to 1896. Between 1870 and 1910, Legal History was offered only three times, and Roman Law only twice.[7] Langdell's goal was to sever law from the academy, to insulate it from more humanistic fields of study such as political science, sociology, anthropology, literature, and history. Ironically, this anti-intellectual stance insured the law school's acceptance into the academy. This was due to the ascendancy of empiricism and the scientific method, which came to dominate American universities in the late nineteenth century. As one historian put it, "Virtually no one today challenges the propriety of the law school's place in the university. The achievement is Langdell's greatest contribution to both legal education and legal history. . . . He made it an inductive science at a time when the idea of a university, and indirectly knowledge itself was being similarly secularized in terms of the scientific method."[8]

Langdell might have disapproved of my historical bent, Deborah, but he would have gone berserk over your insistence on finding hidden issues of class and race in every contracts case ever written. Auerbach argues that Langdell's view of law study as a science in which doctrinal analysis and inductive reasoning define "thinking like a lawyer" has allowed legal educators to turn their backs on questions about the relationship between law and justice. Auerbach also sees Langdell's ideas as consistent with the general trend in American education in the late nineteenth century—to seek security from fear of social disorder in scientific expertise. "Science," Auerbach wrote, "became the metaphor for reason and order to quell apprehension about urban, labor, and racial unrest."[9] A century later, the same claims of value-free neutrality are still made in the law school. As Auerbach put it, "The baby is now one hundred years old, but the cradle still rocks and the soothing hands of doctrinal logic still do the rocking."[10] It is no quirk of fate that I feel uncomfortable with Perry's final stage of Commitment, when professorial neutrality is touted as a virtue, and many law teachers are committed to not being committed.

And let's face it, Deborah, Christopher Columbus Langdell would hate our being in the classroom at all. He wanted to exclude women from the scientific enterprise of studying law. A petition was presented to the Harvard Law School in 1889 to admit women to the law school, and the faculty voted that if Radcliffe were willing to accept a woman as a graduate student, then the law school would permit her to take courses and exams. Langdell dissented, and I am sure that, despite the favorable vote from the rest of the faculty, he was not alone in wanting to keep us out. I know he wasn't. Ezra Ripley Thayer, who later became the dean of the law school, expressed "the view of all the others when he said that he should regret the presence of a woman in his classes, because he feared it might affect the excellence of the work of the men; but he could not deny the inherent justice of the claim."[11]

I am certain that Langdell did not intend it, but the schizophrenia he created with the Socratic method—this gap between classroom and examination coverage—has given law teachers tremendous freedom. He created a tradition of not covering the course material in class, and in that carved out space of institutionalized irrelevance, you and I are at liberty to wander. We cross the boundaries of foreign lands that Langdell would never have approved of. We may get criticized for our choice of destinations, but no one ever suggests that we should have stayed home.

And we do get criticized, Deborah, by students and colleagues alike. It's not only the substance of what we choose to talk about that offends, but also how we choose to talk about it. We both of us embroider our classroom narratives with asides, and asides of asides. How many times have I heard it said that you "digress" in class and "go off on tangents"? Or that I am "flaky" or "ditsy"? An article I read last summer gave me some insight into why our mode of discourse garners criticism. In a study of the narratives of litigants in small claims court, O'Barr and Conley distinguish between a rule-oriented account and a relationship account:

> A relationship account emphasizes status and relationships, and is organized around the litigant's efforts to introduce these issues into trial. A rule-oriented account emphasizes rules and laws, and is tightly structured around these issues. . . . Rule-oriented accounts mesh better with the logic of the law and the courts. They . . . concentrate on the issues that the court is likely to deem relevant to the case. . . . By contrast, relational accounts are filled with background details that are presumably relevant to the litigant, but not necessarily to the court, and emphasize the complex web of relationships between the litigants rather than the legal rules or formal contracts.[12]

According to O'Barr and Conley, rule-oriented logic is associated with powerful groups, and socially powerless speakers use relational logic in their testimony. Guess which group we belong to?

So not only do we challenge the still dominant view that law is a neutral science, but we sound weird doing it. In O'Barr and Conley's terms, our narratives are relational, not rule-oriented. Background materials matter; social context matters. I do not consider these "tangents" at all. My dictionary says a tangent is a "change of course," but who said we were going somewhere in the first place? People who talk about "going off on a tangent" are the same people who believe in "arriving at the right answer." Neither of us wants to promote the belief that the law has any "right" answers—instead, it has a lot of different answers. Furthermore, in the grander scheme of things the law is not the only source of answers. So many who are associated with "powerful groups" regard the law as a "jealous mistress." But in our view, she is one among many interesting guests one might invite to a party—worthy of talking to and taking into consideration, but not to the exclusion of all others. Jealousy is the wrong metaphor.

I think my lack of solemnity about the law is particularly disturbing to my students and colleagues. I simply refuse to take the "law part" of anything too seriously, because I think the "law part" is just that: a part. And so I poke fun at the law a lot, and shrug my shoulders a lot, and say that I don't know a lot, and on occasion even say that I don't care. The form that my public assertions takes is threatening. Aisenberg and Harrington, in their fascinating book about women in academia, write about feminine discourse in the classroom:

> But by not adopting the male model of professional speech, women may not be manifesting a lack of serious address to their disciplines. Rather, they may be challenging old modes of authority—rejecting authoritative assertion as the mode for pur-

suing knowledge and expressing it. The tentativeness of their speaking style may express a belief that what can be known *is* more tentative than firm assertion makes it seem.[13]

There are messages sent in our discursive styles, Deborah, and I think a lot of students, and some of our colleagues, think your "tangents" and my casualness manifest disrespect for the law. They are wrong, of course. We do have respect for the law, but only the respect it is due as one piece of a much larger puzzle.

After the retreat, I found myself wondering whether these messages have had the wrong effect on that hardworking intelligent person who did not understand what the task was, that person who did not do well on my exam. On that student's behalf, and in recognition that my teaching style sent mixed signals, I decided to take Lee Knefelkamp's advice at the retreat and be more explicit about the kinds of tasks involved in Property and my methods of assessment. I was not promising to cure the schizophrenia, but at least I would try to disclose the nature of the disease.

Once I started to analyze the cognitive tasks involved in Property, I was somewhat appalled. At least a third of the student's brainpower needed to be spent performing a set of fairly mundane tasks: understanding, organizing, and memorizing the doctrines. Augustine, or any of Perry's Dualists, would have been in heaven. In small pockets of Property, there actually *are* right answers—in future interests, the rule against perpetuities, assignments, and subleases, to name a few. This material represented, at least in part, the doctrinal competence and technical expertise that I had been silently expecting.

In order to communicate the value I attached to the mastery of these doctrines, I prepared a set of handouts which included definitions, rules, exceptions, and so forth, and sometimes a technical explanation. Then I told the students for the very first time, here it is; you have to learn this stuff. I will test you on it, probably with multiple-choice questions, even if we do not talk about it in class. You cannot survive the course without demonstrating your mastery of this material.

Some of the handouts were quite elegant, with charts and arrows and enumeration, indicating a beginning and an end. They were so neat and tidy that looking at them, no one would suspect there could ever be anything messy or contradictory about the law presented. My students really loved them, and I worried about that—and still do. There are dangers lurking in those handouts. They bear a latent jurisprudential message about the certainty and autonomy of the law, a message that by and large I do not want to send. As Thomas Eisele wrote in his wonderful essay on Wittgenstein:

> Telling you what I want you to learn or know may be efficient or economical in conveying my message, and these are important values in education. Sometimes, too, this may be the best way of getting the message across, of getting the students to learn the lesson I wish them to learn. But for all its effi-

ciency and economy and "precision," this mode of address has its costs, and pedagogically speaking, they can be steep. Teaching by telling may convey finished thoughts or ideas explicitly, but its very explicitness and the "finish" of the ideas may make it too "clean" an educational process for its own good—or, rather, for the good of the students. . . . An explicit message (no matter how precise) may sometimes be a misleading message, because it is an inaccurate or inadequate expression of what is known or intended.[14]

Still, despite the dangers Eisele warned of, I have decided that I am willing to risk sending the wrong message about the nature of law in order to transmit information regarding certain discrete areas of Property. Consider the rule against perpetuities, a highly technical rule prohibiting testators from imposing conditions on the use of their property for too many generations. The rule against perpetuities is not an area of law that I would choose to teach, but the pressures from the outside world have forced it upon me. All those who seek the privilege of practicing law have to know the rule against perpetuities, although after the bar exam, most lawyers quickly let its details slide into the river of sludge that runs through the unconscious. The rule remains in those dense waters, but it can be dredged up if needed, and even the knowledge of its existence, the awareness that it is down there to worry about, can make the difference between a competent lawyer and a sloppy one.

And so I am willing to bear some of the costs of sending the dreaded message that the law is neat and tidy, at least with respect to these technical areas of law that are the subject of my elegant handouts. I feel I have taken care of that deeper problem in my course—the problem of notice to my students that they are responsible for this material. No one can now claim ignorance of the requirement of doctrinal competence for the exam, nor for that matter—if they absorb the contents of the handout—can they claim ignorance of the doctrines.

A second component of doctrinal competence that I wanted to put my students on notice of involved the use of Knefelkamp's level 3, Late Multiplicity tasks. It is not enough to have learned the principles, rules, and definitions. The students need to know what to do with them. Again, following Knefelkamp's advice, I have begun to say to my class, over and over again: I do not care what your conclusion is, only how you arrived at it. Take responsibility for your answers. Probably the most valuable thing I did was to give a midterm exam, worth only 25 percent of the grade, and in assessing an essay on landlord/tenant law I spilled the blood of a dozen pens on their papers, telling them what they had done wrong, and praising their work when they got it right.

During class, I then took an hour in the middle of the semester to show them a sample A answer, a sample B answer, and a sample C answer. I told them I wanted the papers to show a sensitivity to the sources of law, from the oldest layers of common law to the newest legislative gloss, and to recognize the interrelationships among these competing authorities. I expected arguments to follow a logical sequence; rules to be stated before exceptions; tests and standards to be articulated before being applied. I expected difficult terms to be defined and analyzed. In application, I expected the student to ferret out relevant facts from red herrings. I expected the landlord's position to be fully explored, and the tenant's as well. I expected the student to be able to assess the strengths and weaknesses of the different arguments, and to explain why the landlord might be doomed, or why he might prevail. These criteria are no surprise to any teacher of law, or to any successful taker of law school exams. In our profession they constitute a road map of how to arrive at a "better" opinion, and as with all Late Multiplicity tasks, the actual location at arrival is irrelevant; what matters is how you got there.

Besides saying publicly at least once during the semester what the criteria were for excellence on the exam, the sacrifice of a dozen red pens was the most important part of the midterm exercise. For most of my students, that midterm exam in Property turned out to be the only exam that was ever handed back to them. Legal education has such bizarre pedagogical customs. We do not test our students throughout their first year, and then the entire assessment of their ability and mastery of the material is jammed into one grueling exam they never see again. Unless they struggle to make an appointment several months later for the ritual of "going over the exam"—and few do— the recipients of those grades are kept in the dark about how they were arrived at. This practice is the very antithesis of good level 3, Late Multiplicity work. We just send the conclusion out to them, encoded in a letter grade, with no hints as to how, or whether, we arrived at it responsibly.

There was nothing on the exam, either the midterm or the final, that required any Commitment-level thought. Neither was there anything on the exam that reflected much of that part of Property I love to talk about: the jurisprudence of it, its poetic qualities, the psychology of litigation between neighbors, and, of course, its long and fascinating history. I decided to assign a ten-page paper, toward the end of the semester, to be completed within a month to count as 25 percent of the grade. The topic was to present and apply at least one theory of property to one of a smorgasbord of peculiar circumstances: the discovery of pre-Celtic coins in a farmer's field in England;[15] the unearthing of the bones of 420 colonial slaves in downtown Manhattan;[16] the disposition of dinosaur bones in the Black Hills of South Dakota;[17] the division of a graduate degree when love had dried up and blown away.[18]

In assigning the paper, I was partly motivated by a desire to rescue that intelligent, hardworking student who did not understand the nature of the task on the final exam. Here, I thought, was a place to reward a breadth of knowledge and imagination. Here too was a time for the student to pick and choose his words with care. Unlike successful blue book writing, which requires short-term retention and expulsion of doctrine, a paper calls for introspection and precision. I was also partly motivated by a desire to make those literal-minded students, the ones who shut down whenever I discussed material-that-would-not-be-covered-on-the-exam, stay awake in class. For this quarter of the course, I put together my own materials, some from the canon—Locke and Hobbes—and others from law reviews. I then scheduled an hour at least every three weeks to formally discuss some of the underlying theories of property. It was the first time I had officially set aside class time for profundity. Schedules reflect and communicate values, and before this experiment, ideas in my Property class were smuggled in through the back door as random, unannounced visitors. Now ideas were to enter through the front door, invited guests, to be treated with honor and respect.

When I got around to grading the papers, I was very satisfied. They were all respectable, and many were exceptional. Everyone grappled with a theory of property, and tried to apply it, and many were able to decide who should get the treasure trove, the future earnings, or the bones of ancient reptiles or lost human beings. Since I have such doubts myself about Commitment, I was loathe to demand it of others, but many of my students were clearly committed, and expressed it eloquently, unsolicited. With both the English coins and the *Tyrannosaurus rex,* the students had to resolve the tension between private ownership and the public's desire and need to have access to these rare and precious things.

The article I had given them regarding the largest and earliest collection of African American remains made several suggestions about what could be done with the bones, including pouring concrete over them, moving them, or making a museum on the site. I discovered that there was no way to write about this problem without confronting one's beliefs about the cruel history of the people who were buried in that small corner of Manhattan, and the cruel history of their descendants, many of whom were writing the essays. This problem also required students to own up to their attitudes about death, burial, and how and why we owe a duty to the dead. Many students did not find a traditional theory of property to protect the burial site, and the best papers dealt with why that might be so. In reading them, I was reminded of an insight I have treasured from Jack Himmelstein: "Some of the most enlightening and rewarding moments for me as an educator have come when a student, perplexed by a day's learning, suddenly discovered that his or her 'problem' lay not in lack of abilities but in knowing more than the limited frameworks we had been applying had allowed." [19] No one seemed able to find a doctrine to rescue the remains of these enslaved people, those skeletons that somehow belonged to them; and the recognition that the legal and philosophical framework was limited sobered them. It felt like, and indeed was, another instance of not mattering.

The most emotionally charged papers were those that dealt with the problem of whether graduate degrees should be the subject of marital property. Here was an issue close to *their* bones. Almost no one argued both sides of this question; commitment came naturally. John Locke's theory could be worn with elegance by either the diligent student-spouse or the diligent supporting spouse, and almost always it was lined with the satin of hidden hostility. In reading these papers, I worried about the state of some of their marriages. The problem forced the students to confront the law of property as a form of social ordering, with foundations in political theory and hidden values that had nothing to do with the cool abstraction of legal thought. And in some instances, the problem forced the students to confront their spouses, and the sacrifices being made for them to attend law school.

Some students hated having to write a paper, particularly those who excelled at short-term retention and expulsion of doctrine, but most students enjoyed the opportunity to express themselves in their own language, and the freedom to experience confusion and seek its resolution without devastation. As I had anticipated, several of the marginal students who were not performing well on exams flourished in the take-home essay format. A few managed to rescue themselves, avoiding academic dismissal, and I was able to divest myself of our mutual failure. In fact, for me as a teacher, taking the advice of a specialist in cognitive theory was a resounding success.

But for me as a person, and particularly as a writer, it was a resounding failure. The grading almost crushed me. I already had twenty long papers to critique and grade from my Jurisprudence class, and forty short reflection pieces from the same course, plus the ninety blue books from Property. The additional weight of ninety ten-page papers was more than I could bear.

Unlike the mind-numbing, routine, and rhythmic grading of blue books, these papers required my full attention. Each one represented hours of human effort. I could not approach them with indifference. I did not know how to take their words lightly, and so had to bear them heavily, subject to the earth's terrible pull of gravity.

The grading went on, week after week, month after month, and all my glorious summer time in which to write evaporated into thin air. It was a desperate feeling, to watch the hours of each day slip away, paper by paper. I felt as if I were moving through molasses, and no matter how diligent I intended to be, the time allotted was never enough. The trip to see Dan's parents in Ireland at the end of July was originally intended as a reward for finishing an article. Instead, I just barely finished grading the papers before crossing the Atlantic. In Ireland, against a backdrop of lush green, I was haunted by the specter of unfulfilled summer dreams and unkept promises, and disappointment over words never written. The worst thing about the situation was my lack of standing to mourn. I had done all this to myself; there was no one to blame but me.

I have since acquired some distance from the situation. Time has lifted the blame for the lost summer off my shoulders. When I raised my head to look around, I found myself angry, senselessly angry—about anything in my profession that I could find to be angry about.

I find myself wondering why there were ninety students in my Property class in the first place. Teaching should be an intimate relationship, one where a great deal of energy is exchanged between two people. Lecturing in our moot court room is like trying to illuminate a cavernous roller skating rink with a hundred-watt bulb. All those faces looking out at me from the dark corners of the room, searching for a source of light. I can see that those faces bear eyes, but I never get to look into them.

And then, why did I have to grade all those damn blue books? A friend of mine teaches in a large state university, and he can't believe that we don't have teaching assistants to help with the routine grading. Why is it taboo to even suggest that someone other than a professor be the initial reader of law school exams? I am not suggesting that we turn the entire grading process over to the teaching assistants, only portions of the process. My friend who teaches large undergraduate introductory courses described his standard operating procedure. He meets with the TAs to explain and distribute a model answer. The TAs all go home and grade their stack of blue books, making written comments on an assessment form designed by the professor. The professor then reads each exam and reviews the TAs' comments and recommended assessment. He then meets with each TA to go over problematic exams. The grade is initially suggested by the TA, but then must be ratified by the professor. My friend insists that the use of TAs not only saves him precious time, but gives the student a much more thorough and fair assessment of his work.

Some have suggested that such a system would save little time.[20] I described the procedure to one of my colleagues who said, "Gee, if I had to make up a model answer and draft an assessment form, and then have to read all the exams anyhow, I would just as soon put a grade on them myself." I was shocked. It seems to me that any grader should make up a model answer for an exam, draft an assessment sheet that reflects what is being tested for and whether the exam taker met the norm, make written comments, and be able to justify each grade based on these comments. I was shocked, but I should not have been. Every semester, it takes me several weeks to grade my exams, while my colleague turns his grades in after several days.

In several different forums, I have tried to bring up the suggestion that we use TAs to help us grade, only to have the idea summarily and hastily rejected. Why is it such a threatening suggestion? Do we really believe that the difference between a contingent remainder and a vested remainder subject to complete divestment is so esoteric that only a law professor can master it? Does it undermine our mystique as the purveyors of secret knowledge to share the burden of grading exams? I for one would gladly exchange mystique for some freedom.

And how have I come to place such a high value on my writing? What exactly is my job supposed to be? I started teaching, as most of us do, because I wanted to be a teacher. A decade later, I only want to be a writer. While I do not demean my current aspirations—they are heartfelt—I do wonder how they happened. Of one thing I am certain: it was not my idea. As the years went by, the Promotion and Tenure Committee kept sending me memoranda expressing concern about the snail-like progress of my scholarship. The message was loud and clear: Yes, yes, you seem to be a good teacher, but where are those law review articles?

To my mind, the world would be a better place without

all those law review articles. Most legal scholarship is engaged in to keep our jobs or to win local or global approval. A lot of trees have been sacrificed needlessly in the name of scholarship, and a lot of time and talent wasted that could have been spent on more socially useful endeavors. This is particularly true of most scholars' early works, written to achieve tenure. The requirement that a new teacher acquire mastery of the subject matter of new courses, learn how to teach, and write at least two "tenure pieces" within five years has resulted in a lot of redundant, thorough, and unread law review articles.

No one seems to care if these tenure pieces are about anything interesting or important. Consider this description of the advice that is casually tossed at new law teachers:

> The new professor is left even more adrift where scholarship is concerned. Should a major piece be undertaken first or a shorter, simpler one? Short and simple to start. Will writing on legal education, a clinical topic, or women's rights be regarded as "nonscholarly"? Probably. Should I write alone or with a co-author for my first article? Alone. Should I do a casebook or an article first? An article.[21]

Why would we want to encourage new scholars to tackle only short, simple issues? What is wrong with complex, ambitious projects? Why would we want to steer new scholars away from topics like legal education, when that is supposed to be our avocation? Who decided that women's issues, which affect over half the human race, are on the B list? (Answer: people who are on the A list.) What is wrong with collaboration? When I read formulae like these, I am so grateful to my grandmother for having given so much bad, gratuitous advice during my childhood. In resisting her will, I learned the fine art of ignoring the bad, gratuitous advice of others.

But let's face it: when the Promotion and Tenure Committee is sending you dire memoranda suggesting that your job is on the line, it is hard to be sturdy. So I wrote a few of those law review articles, and the most amazing thing happened: I became seduced by words and ideas. Now all I want to do is read and write. The teacher in me has begun to disappear, and when she came back to me last summer, I resented the intrusion. I came to writing because I wanted to keep teaching, but now I teach only so that I can keep writing.

I see now that our project was not a failed mission, but a misunderstood one—misunderstood by me at least. I thought we would learn how to challenge our students, and ended up being the one who was challenged. When I read the materials on cognitive theory, the ideas all made perfect sense to me. But in the process of trying to take them seriously, to put them into action, I discovered architectural barriers from the structure of my own life—a life I had built for myself, with purpose and perhaps commitment. It was a revelation—I did not even know the walls were there.

And so, Deborah, I have done what I said I would do: I told you the story of my experiment with the Knefelkamp and Perry scheme of cognitive development. As I said, it was a success. My Property course has been made better for the effort, my students benefited, and will benefit in the future, particularly if I ever have the strength to assign papers again. But the questions that emerged from the fury of my anger were the unexpected treasures. Those questions about legal education are important ones, I think, and that one about how to be a scholar without losing the face may even be profound.

SIX

Fall

🍂

SORTING BULBS BEFORE PLANTING

I became anxious in the middle of the afternoon on the first day of our retreat. We were still talking about learning. We were running out of time before we'd begun to discuss teaching. I went up to Lee Knefelkamp after her presentation and asked quietly, "Excuse me, how do we get our students from stage 1 to stage 4?" She smiled enigmatically and took my hand in hers, giving it a little squeeze of comfort. Moments later she was off to Manhattan, and

I was standing in a lovely inn feeling a sense of terrible loss.

I recognized the source of my apprehension. I wanted an answer. I wanted Lee Knefelkamp to explain what we were supposed to do with the information she had given us. I needed instructions, a manual for transforming my classroom. I wanted someone with authority to tell me the right answer. Even as I asked for help, I made a mental note, a silent confession. I acknowledged my regression to that anathema of all contemporary educators, Dualism. Saying that one is a Dualist is probably the equivalent of saying that one is simpleminded. Those who write about learning always refer to Dualism in a disparaging way. Pity the poor people stuck in Dualism who "cannot comprehend when addressed relativistically and panic."[1] It is humiliating, losing ground this way, and cold comfort to be told that learning is an "ego-threatening" process, especially at this stage in our lives.[2]

To be honest, I don't know if I am up to any task which threatens my ego. Remember how thrilled I was a few years ago when you used me in one of your classes as an example of a person who lives in the world of ideas? I was thrilled because you recognized me as an intellectual. (Am I correct in believing that this is what you meant by living in the world of ideas?) I was thrilled because there are some who think that Blacks do not inhabit that world, that they cannot even reach it. I was thrilled because it had been a long time since someone remarked on my mind and not my personal skills, my empathy or my humor or gregariousness. I was tired of being nice. I wanted to hear that I was bright.

Louise, I want you to know that I consider this a risky enterprise, and the extent of the risk has recently become more obvious. Cognitive theory has been invoked by those who seek to prove that Black people are inferior to white people. In the literature we read on cognitive theory, we have seen how this could be so. There are repeated references to the cultural construct "intelligence," which is at the heart of theories of racial superiority. Howard Gardner describes the meaning we assign to this idea:

> Those who view all intellect as a piece . . . not only believe in a singular, inviolable capacity which is the special property of human beings: often, as a corollary, they impose the conditions that each individual is born with a certain amount of intelligence, and that we individuals can in fact be rank ordered in terms of our God given intellect or I.Q. So entrenched is this way of thinking—and talking—that most of us lapse readily into rankings of individuals as more or less "smart," "bright," "clever," or "intelligent." [3]

The explanation alludes to the deeper and more dangerous meanings hidden within this invitation to comparison. Over and over again, exclusion and deprivation and physical injury are justified by "scientific" proof of the inferiority of people of color. Darwin has to take some of the responsibility. The idea of "natural selection" is so powerful that the mere mention of his name is enough to lend credibility to even the most outlandish theory. And it is the idea of "natural selection," or our need to create a system that controls for the lack of "natural selection" among humans, that is used by advocates of eugenics, old and new. No one should be surprised that even today Black women are sterilized more often than white women [4] or that eugenic theories continue to be embraced by those who argue that race and intellect are linked genetically. Ego-threatening is an understatement in this context.

I have another confession to make. I know every score I ever received on any test that I thought would measure my intelligence or my intellectual worth. I know my IQ, my SAT scores, my LSAT scores. Even though I reject their validity and am outraged that anyone would think that our worth as human beings could be reduced to a simple number, I hang on to these numbers for dear life. They are proof of my worth in a world that thinks intelligence can be quantified; they are proof that the generalizations about Blacks are wrong; they are my protection against poverty or sterilization.

Charles Murray is all over the media these days being interviewed about *The Bell Curve*.[5] I think of him as an entrepreneurial scholar, one who has identified a market demand and exploited it profitably. He has capitalized on the tenacity of the idea of racial superiority. Anyone who looked carefully would see this is an idea that is cyclical in its popularity; it comes around once each generation as a matter of "scholarly" debate. Charles Murray is the darling of television talk show hosts, but his interviews are carefully choreographed to avoid any real challenge to the *a priori* assumptions of this theory. The entertainment value of these programs would be diminished if anyone ever made him defend the meaning he assigns to "intelligence."

Charles Murray is always asked about his own IQ, and he is always allowed to avoid the question. He doesn't know his IQ, but Dick Herrnstein, his deceased collaborator, did. With a smug smile, Charles Murray says he thinks his own IQ is very high, which would make him, by his own description, "very smart."

I am no Charles Murray. I cannot sit in a chair being interviewed and say, "Well, I assume I am very smart." A coy smile and a wry answer will not do. I am compelled to answer: my last IQ test score was 132, my SAT scores in my senior year were 709 verbal and 580 math. The year before, I scored 643 in math. My LSAT score was 163 and I placed in the ninety-ninth percentile in writing ability. Oh, go on, you say, no one would ever ask you that! But I have been asked during a job interview whether I was Phi Beta Kappa as an undergraduate. I also was asked for my LSAT scores. So perhaps now you will understand why I still have the faded and yellow piece of paper with my LSAT scores on it. I keep it in case my word isn't good enough. I also had an unofficial copy of my transcript from law school, but I gave it to the person who interviewed me for my first teaching job. I'm not one to forget what I learned as an anthropology major in college: "the step from science to mythology is short and all too attractive."[6] I read the current and continuing debate in academia over who is qualified to teach and how we measure the quality of scholarship in a particular historical context. The power of myths about intellectual superiority and inferiority cannot be ignored.

You will understand, Louise, my sensitivity around this issue and my unwillingness to experiment with a theory I didn't understand. That would be an invitation to disaster. And if I have been ungracious when others thought they were complimenting me, it is because I envy the spontaneous exclamations your work excites, the references to your brilliance.

A few years ago, I might have laughed at the suggestion that I am anything other than practical, with feet firmly planted on the ground, eyes focused on the tangible objects of this world. But even then I would have had to admit that although there has never been a time when I was uncomfortable with ideas, there have been ideas with which I was uncomfortable—ideas I could not grasp and theories that seemed opaque and incomprehensible to me. I struggle still with some of these ideas, trying to decipher the language of the current debate and the way names are used as shorthand for ideas: Derrida, Foucault, Habermas, Wittgenstein. And in the past year, I have been struggling to digest the theories that abound in the field of cognitive science, theories that have a particular and peculiar relevance for me. The surprise has been how much I *enjoy* the struggle.

After the retreat, I gave up on the idea of experimenting in the classroom with the Perry scheme. You could say I went backward rather than forward. I began by questioning Perry's basic assumption that even in higher education, there is a developmental process involved. Does the way we think change over time? I had only my own experience with learning to measure the truth of Perry's theory. I worried about the legitimacy of my methodology, but I have been assured that cognitive science has its roots in both science and philosophy.[7] Introspection was in exile during the ascendancy of behaviorism in the sciences, but it has been welcomed back and is valid here. We are in the realm of metacognition, where we are free to think about the way we think, to think about how our thinking has changed over time.

The reservations I have about Perry's theory are grounded in my suspicion that if my thinking is more complex, richer, or more textured than it was when I was younger, it is the result of a natural process of accretion. I simply know more now than I did then. If I have moved beyond Dualism, it is not because I learned how to think contextually, but because I have more context with which to work. If my thinking has changed over the years, the difference may be the amount of time I spend in the domain of metathought, thinking about thinking. Metathought is the name Perry gives to the process by which we reconcile our contradictory or conflicting commitments, the tension created by our ability to accept ourselves as both "tentative" and "wholehearted" in those commitments. Metathought is dialectical thought or logic, although Perry is careful to distinguish his use of the term "dialectic" from the use of the term by Marx, Hegel, and Nietzsche. Perry believes that dialectic is "characteristic of the higher ranges of human development," and dialectic is not just Dualism because it involves "forward transcendent movement."[8]

I can't deny the fact that I have experienced learning as a kind of movement—mostly, but not always, a forward movement. For instance, in my law practice, I felt as though my brain had started to atrophy. If it had not been for spirited debates with one of my colleagues I think my mind might have perished a little at a time. It would have passed away unnoticed and unmourned during one of those late-night meetings at the printers where we sat "slugging lines" to make sure no paragraph had fallen out of a document while it was being printed.

I recall my own learning as erratic, not smooth. I experienced the most noticeable leaps while I was in college, law school, and later after I began teaching and writing. I associate the first leap with the revelation that there are taxonomies that make the world comprehensible, that these taxonomies are our own invention, so natural to us as the creators that it is hard to imagine a world organized in any other way.

In college, I began to see—or to have pointed out to me—an unending list of dichotomies between science and art, reason and emotion, truth and beauty. I recall my first self-conscious examination of this system of binary opposition and modernist ideals. The occasion was my introduction to Stephen Daedalus in a course called Philosophy of the Novel. I plodded through his long monologue explaining his aesthetic theory, the differences between dramatic emotion and aesthetic emotion, between kinetic or improper art and beauty; the relationships between Truth and Beauty and Good and Evil.[9] In law school, these oppositions took on a new meaning as we talked about the dichotomy between reason and emotion in Constitutional Law.

Now that I am in teaching, I find myself knee-deep in categories and oppositions, reading the work of scholars like Jay Feinman—for whom I have a particular fondness because he always seems to be just one step ahead of me in "finding" and exploring the topics that interest me, like taxonomies and pedagogy, power and politics. I think Feinman is wrong, though, when he suggests that the law cannot survive without classifications or paradigms: "the unreality of this suggestion [that we engage in a particularized determination of each case without benefit of categories or paradigms] is apparent in its statement; a doctrinal system without doctrinal categories is neither practical nor law as we know it."[10] Why should it be impractical?

As soon as someone pointed to the conceptual taxonomies, the oppositions that we use to organize life, I knew I was being invited to disagree. I don't know whether I was in college or graduate school when I stumbled across Phaedrus and his discussion of the "problem of stuckness," which he explained was "traditional rationality's insistence upon 'objectivity,' a doctrine that there is a divided reality of subject and object."[11] Of course, Phaedrus was talking about a motorcycle most of the time, but that didn't matter. What did matter was the suggestion he made that we abandon duality. "This eternally dualistic subject-object way of approaching the motorcycle sounds right to us because we're used to it. But it's not right. It's always been an artificial interpretation superimposed on reality."[12]

I feel at home with those who were skeptical about duality, like Phaedrus, because my life proves the insignificance and the power of dualities. I am one of those people who fall between categories. Today they would say I am "mixed race" or "multiracial," but back when I was in college there were fewer choices. Whether you were mulatto, an octaroon, or a person with one drop of Black blood, you were Black. Despite the existence of terms meant to describe gradations of blackness, the classificatory scheme used in American society is or was binary. You were Black or white, nothing in between.[13]

There is a great short story by Langston Hughes, "Who's Passing for Who?" that describes the indeterminacy I understand and live as a member of a community that sees and understands complexity, even the complexity created by an opposition that fails in its essential purpose. Hughes's narrator recounts his experience with a couple whose status was ambiguous. "We just stood there on the corner in Harlem dumbfounded—not knowing now which way we'd been fooled. Were they really white—passing for colored? Or colored, passing for white? Whatever race they were, they had too much fun at our expense—even if they did pay for the drinks."[14]

Like Langston Hughes, I learned to question categories, to see the way the lines blur. And in college, because I was allowed to question categories, I was able to consider whether they fit my own sense of the world; I was free to think about reorganizing the world in ways I thought reasonable, logical, and consistent with my own epistemologies.

In my own field, the law, I am perfectly comfortable taking theories apart and putting them together again, using what I know from my lived experience and what I have learned as a student of the law to critique theories. Over the years I have gained a sense of my own competence and confidence in my own intellectual ability. But I have been brought up short by this project. The intellectual free fall that occurs when you abandon a preferred taxonomy or paradigm in a field you "know" is nothing like the panic I experienced when I first realized I would be held accountable for knowing cognitive theory.

This is singularly different from the experience of ignorance, from the realization that you do not know something. Do you remember the Critical Race Theory Conference we went to in Madison in 1990? We walked around the cold streets and you kept a watchful eye out for the Louise who attended Wisconsin as an undergraduate. You gave me a tour that included Ann Emery Hall, Home for Girls of Good Breeding, the dorm from which you had been evicted for behavior inappropriate for a young lady. I looked carefully for a younger version of you in the window you pointed out. At that conference we attended panel discussions of postmodernism and poststructuralism without a clue as to what either of them meant. Don't you remember? And last year we spent two days at a conference listening to people talk about someone named Lacan, a scholar whose writings we had missed somehow. It didn't matter how much we knew or didn't know, because we were there to listen and learn. We were comfortable in our ignorance and excited about learning.

The first day of our faculty retreat was a qualitatively different experience. The retreat was not an opportunity to combine virtue and pleasure, a stroll along the bank of some river of knowledge during which we exercise our minds and indulge our natural curiosity. This had more the feel of a forced march, and I wanted to know where I was going and how long, approximately, it would take me to get there. For months afterward as I read through the literature, I found myself looking for that simple answer, a road map, even as I was being hypnotized by the complexity of the material.

Lee Knefelkamp began with Perry's scheme, but I quickly wandered away. I sought an overview of the field and found it in Howard Gardner's history of cognitive science. I had not realized that we were about to begin work in a field that is the subject of some controversy until I read that the "construct of the mind" is thought by some "to do more harm than good."[15] According to Gardner, cognitive science is positioned between science and the humanities, between the scientists who concern themselves with biology, with the brain and neurological structures,[16] and those who concern themselves with behavior, the affective and cultural branch of cognitive theory explored by disciplines like sociology, anthropology, and psychology.

I am pretty clear which branch we're on, but even after you locate yourself in intellectual space, you still have to decide where you want to go next. I missed the chance for a spring planting, but I have until the first frost to plant bulbs that should bloom in the spring. I have been given a second chance, but I need to figure out where to begin. Sorting bulbs and deciding where I will place jonquils and tulips and daffodils, where I want a swatch of orange or red or bright yellow, seems as good a place to start as any. And when I go out in the yard with my plan in my head, I will have to turn over the soil. At which end of the garden should I begin? Lee Knefelkamp included a list in her survey of the field: psychosocial theories, developmental theories, maturity theories, typology theories, and person/environment theories.[17]

I have had to retrace my steps several times, asking myself to "repeat" the question in a manner that reminds me of my own first-year Contracts students. How do I move my students from stage 1 to stage 4? I remind myself that my problem is the project of all those, like Perry, who labor in the field of learning theory. It is a matter of some concern for those who dwell on either branch of cognitive theory, science or humanities. Those who equate the operation of our brains with information processing, for instance, have isolated two different areas for study: one is the way the brain works while it is at a particular point in the developmental scheme—in what Perry describes as a position or stage. The other more difficult area is explaining how transition is made from one stage to another. What makes it difficult is that these scientists have to assume that the information processing system (which is our mind) has the capacity to "modify its own structure."[18]

That is my problem exactly. As a teacher, I am encouraged by Perry's description of the student who has moved from concentration to thinking, who has changed his or her epistemological assumptions about learning. It is possible to make a student see that books are read for the ideas they contain, or because he or she has an interest in them, not because an instructor says "read these." Learning is presented as an attainable goal. But I want to know the mechanics; I want to know how students can modify the structure of their minds so they can think in new and different ways and how I help them do this.

Perry's reference to "the strategies which we invite our students to learn" looks like a clue. I have concluded that Perry is referring, although he doesn't use this term, to what others have labeled "critical thinking." This requires a leap, of course, to the literature that renames and fleshes out this cognitive ideal.[19] But what is most intriguing about this literature is the promise that critical thinking can be taught.

One of the scholars in the field of critical thinking calls his version of the Perry scheme a taxonomy. In accordance with the scientific tradition, the taxonomy is named after the person who discovered it, someone named Bloom.[20] Bloom's taxonomy is a hierarchy of educational behavior with "cumulative properties."

Even though Perry doesn't use the term "critical thinking," I could probably justify the association I have drawn merely by comparing the description of the highest form of thinking in the taxonomy of critical thinking and the meaning assigned to learning at stage 4 of the Perry scheme. In Bloom's taxonomy, for instance, the learner moves from knowledge to comprehension to application to analysis to synthesis to evaluation. Each stage includes its predecessor(s). In Perry's scheme, once the student reaches Contextual Relativism (Commitment), the student can "see complexity, can evaluate, conclude, support his own analysis. Can synthesize, adapt, modify and expand concepts . . . fluidity of thought and analysis. Good with abstraction."[21]

Critical thinking is not a single way of thinking; it is a taxonomy, a list of skills that move from "simple" operations to those that are thought to be more complex in a way which seems more hierarchical than developmental. The Perry scheme is presented as a developmental theory, evolution in a microcosm, which can trace its genealogy to Piaget's biologically based theories. The Piagetian tradition, I have read, assumes movement as children acquire universal and necessary "logicomathematical tools of increasing power." In contrast, critical thinking is a top-down type of theory. It is something people learn to do—students take courses in critical thinking, which promise to teach them how to think better. It can't be natural if it is treated as a field of acquired knowledge.[22]

To put it another way, the Perry scheme feels horizontal while the critical thinking taxonomy feels vertical. When I read Perry's discussion of the stages and the transitions, I pictured a continuum where there were no categories, no clearly demarcated boundaries.

But once Perry has been reduced to four or five stages, and once the focus has been shifted from the transitions to the stages that precede them, there is little to distinguish the two theories. In Perry's scheme, complexity is considered superior to simplicity, and neither Perry nor Knefel-kamp hides the fact that this developmental scheme is "sequential and hierarchical," moving from simpler to more complex thought. All it really takes to see the similarity between Perry's scheme and Bloom's taxonomy is a little manipulation. We have to move Perry's scheme off its back and stand it on its feet.

Perry's developmental scheme	Bloom's taxonomy of educational objectives
Contextual Relativism/Commitment	Evaluation
Late Multiplicity	Analysis
Early Multiplicity	Application
Dualism	Comprehension
"Pure" Dualism	Knowledge

You may wonder, Louise, why I started with critical thinking. Not only was critical thinking the closest to Perry's scheme, it is also something in which I have a personal as well as professional interest. I first encountered the term several years ago when my son transferred from the Amityville School District, a predominantly Black school, to Ocean Avenue School in the Northport School District, a school in which the students of color would be considered statistically insignificant by everyone except their parents. There was a banner in the school that hung in the hallway outside my son's room. It proclaimed in large letters "THINK CRITICALLY!!!"

I happened to see this banner when I was summoned to school to meet with my son's fifth-grade teacher, to respond to her complaints about Christopher. A few days earlier, Christopher had accompanied me to the law school in the evening, as he often did when he was younger and I taught night classes or wished to work late. He did his homework in my office. On that particular evening, he needed paper for his spelling or his English homework and I gave him a white legal pad to use. He wanted loose-leaf paper, but I didn't have any.

When he handed in his homework, his teacher asked him why it was not on white paper. Chris responded, "It is on white paper." She continued to argue with him, insisting that the paper was not white. Most of us recognize this tactic, the literalness of children (or adults) who wish to evade some rule. The appropriate response, the one the teacher finally used, is to tell the student that the interpretive strategy he is using is inappropriate. "You know what I mean" is what she finally said, and she was right.

But the correction came too late. An unflappable ten-year-old had gotten the better of her in front of her students. She marched Chris out into the hall, under the banner that gave him the right to question her definition of white paper, and berated him until he was reduced to tears.

This suggests a certain problem with theories about critical thinking. Not only am I worried about our ability to teach students about "evaluation"; I'm not sure many of our colleagues would be willing to take this chance. Can a scheme succeed that asks a faculty to risk its own authority, even if we are offered the possibility of authority based on trust rather than power as an inducement to take the risk?

We have assumed in our research that the goal of the law professor is the movement of the student along Perry's continuum, but now I am not so sure. How do these taxonomies of thought correlate with the subject matter we teach, law? Should we be teaching our students to think in a particular way, and if so, how does that thinking fit into Perry's scheme? In our reading, I find an article by David Kolb that seems promising. It claims to describe the relationship between academic disciplines and cognitive theory.[23]

Kolb compares various disciplines (or domains) and attempts to catalog cognitive differences among them.[24] His theory is that different disciplines are "tied to theories of logic and cognition" and that there are "pivotal norms" which govern "learning and inquiry" within each profession.[25] I was both amazed and confused by the extensive inventory of thinking processes he developed, a complex set of typologies and categories created to explain the relationship between the way we think, what we are capable of learning, and what we may become.

Kolb has charts and something that looks suspiciously like a graph of statistical results, but the charts are fairly easy to read. Everything moves from right to left and from bottom to top and the oppositions are recognizable: hard and soft, concrete and abstract, applied and active, reflective and pure. The various disciplines are plotted on this graph. Most academics in legal education probably want to find themselves in the quadrant defined by the adjectives "reflective" and "abstract":

concrete (soft)

applied (active)   pure (reflective)

abstract (hard)

According to Kolb, however, the law is not where you would expect to find it. In plotting the position of most disciplines along the line from applied to pure, Kolb reports that nursing is on the reflective side and law on the applied side. Why were nursing, philosophy, and library science all found on the opposite side of the pure/applied divide from law? An inquiry into the methodology of the author explains why. The measure of a discipline's status as applied or pure, it turned out, was the amount of consulting work done by faculty members. This was thought to be a measure of the power the discipline has outside the academic setting. The distinction made no sense to me. I would have measured *applied*-ness in terms of the relationship between the knowledge gained by the students and the use to which that knowledge is put in practice. But the classificatory scheme Kolb describes is more concerned with power than the relationship between knowledge and the usefulness of knowledge.

We have asked how law students learn. It seems appropriate to follow Kolb's suggestion and back up and ask ourselves what it is that lawyers do. It is also probably wise to consider the nature of the inquiry in our profession, and the methodology we use. Kolb asks us to consider the nature of truth in our discipline. We are offered alternatives: does our theory of truth aim at workability or coherence? Do we ask how or why? Are we concerned with events or processes? Do we portray knowledge as action or image? Do we use case studies or historical analysis or field study and clinical observation? In the tradition of our profession, I suppose all these questions are subsumed within the question, "What does it mean to 'think like a lawyer'?"

Kolb's questions, like Perry's stages and Bloom's taxonomy have unsettling implications for our research. If Perry has posited a scheme that is supposed to be universal, why do we spend so much time affirming our desire to teach our students to "think like a lawyer" and then fighting about the content of the curriculum? There is substantial disagreement in our profession about the kind of thinking that should be privileged. Sometimes it is a battle fought over the role of skills and theory in law school training; sometimes it is about the use and misuse of metaphor; sometimes it is about the way an argument is presented, about the relationship between law and the humanities and law and the sciences. If we were to abandon that whole debate, Louise, and merely ask ourselves who will do better on the LSAT, the first-year examinations, and the bar examination—the student at stage 1 or the student at stage 4 in Perry's scheme—what would your answer be?

The problem is I am not sure that all law professors would answer Kolb's questions the same way. There might be significant differences in the responses of law professors, practitioners, and judges. There could be differences of opinion among practitioners who specialize in different fields. The conflict over the meaning assigned to legal education is not something that occurs only in the classroom. The controversy is not limited to the differences in meaning assigned by students and faculty. The entire profession is embroiled in a debate about these very fundamental issues.[26]

What are the truths we teach our students? It is hard to say when in the much smaller universe of the legal academy we disagree about the differences between fact and fiction, art and science, poetry and law, logic and emotion, tradition and innovation, relevance and irrelevance. There is no certainty except the certainty of the oppositional categories we have created, including contradictory attitudes toward knowledge—intellectual elitism and anti-intellectualism.

In some ways, I understand the anger that some law professors and practitioners and judges express at what Judge Harry Edwards has labeled the disjunction between law school and law practice.[27] The tone of his article is aggressive and his portrait of law professors unflattering. I will not gainsay his concern about the lack of preparation law students now receive for practice, but I hear more than that in his anger. I sense that what really bothers him is the social distance that has been established by some members of the legal academy, their sense of superiority, their arrogance, the elitism that infects the whole system.

Louise, I have begun to despair. I was sailing right along, feeling comfortable with the different theories related to cognition until I was asked to relate those theories to what law teachers do. We know there is something called "analysis" and something called "reasoning," but everyone uses a different terminology, expanding and contracting the litany of cognitive skills we wish to impart. To tell you the truth, the best description I've found is one written by Karl Llewellyn in *The Bramble Bush*.[28]

No one assigns this book anymore; I think part of the problem may be the way Llewellyn writes. Students don't have much patience with baroque prose. But Llewellyn's discussion of logic is instructive. It is not only his discussion of inductive and deductive logic that seems relevant to me, but also his discussion of the different kinds of "logical ladders" used by lawyers and judges in particular cases. It is his discussion of the way logic exerts a kind of pressure on judges, and his caveat that judges are not machines that "go mechanically." I read this language with a new appreciation after wading through some of the literature on artificial intelligence and the role it plays in cognitive science, the insights that have been gained by comparing machine logic to human logic. Llewellyn would not be surprised to find that the literature on cognition suggests that all human beings share the characteristics of judges.

We are none of us machines and we are all illogical. We do not "go mechanically." We make judgments, interpreting the facts in a way that machines cannot.[29]

But I think even Llewellyn might be surprised, Louise, to see the extent to which the courts, which write the decisions that appear in our casebooks, and our students have abandoned logic as an ideal. It's as though there has been a massive outbreak of some fantastic disease Derrick Bell might describe in one of his allegories. White men seem to be disproportionately affected with this particular form of incapacity. The white men who contract this disease can't think. Perhaps they never could.

In Contracts class the other day we were comparing and contrasting two cases involving rescues, *Webb v. McGowin* and *Harrington v. Taylor*.[30]

In *Webb,* the promise of the person rescued to pay money to the rescuer was enforced. In *Harrington* it was not. In *Webb,* the person who made the promise had his life saved by a laborer who was injured for life in the process. In *Harrington,* a neighbor was injured when she deflected an ax wielded by a battered woman attempting to decapitate her husband. The husband, who had pursued his fleeing wife into the neighbor's home, promised the neighbor that he would compensate her for the damages she sustained.

My students tried to explain why one promise would be enforced and the other would not, arguing that the second case, *Harrington,* felt less like a contracts case. In fact, both of these cases illustrate the way the lines blur between torts and contract, the public and the private areas of the law respectively. In *Webb,* the court alluded to tort to prove that the value of life can be quantified. And, I told my students, the plaintiff in *Harrington,* who lost her contract action, then brought a suit in tort claiming that the negligence of the husband caused her injury.

"Should she win?" I asked.

One of the men in my class volunteered, "No. She brought her injury on herself."

"But isn't that the case with all rescuers? They don't have to do what they do."

"Her injury was unforseeable."

"Wait a minute," I cautioned, "if a man brings his violence into someone else's home, how can it be unforseeable that a third party might be hurt?"

"But the fight is only between the husband and the wife."

"Isn't it likely that this violence will spill over and hurt someone else?"

"No," he answers. "Besides, if anyone is to blame for the injury to the plaintiff, it is the person wielding the ax. The rescuer had no business interjecting herself into the fight. It was unreasonable for her to do that."

I think a lot about men who think like this. When the cognitive scientists talk about logic, they sometimes describe the " 'semantic principle' which governs inference: a deduction is valid provided there is no way of interpreting the premises correctly that is inconsistent with the conclusion." [31] If the premise in my student's argument is that violence between two parties stays between those two parties and does not affect others, I could think of a number of cases that would be inconsistent with that conclusion. Why couldn't he?

At first I attributed the differences between us to lack of experience, to a lack of knowledge about the real world. Perhaps the student who thought the injury to the neighbor was unforeseeable hadn't been around violence. Maybe he had never seen the way it spills over from a husband to the wife and involves children and in-laws and neighbors. Perhaps he grew up in a place where there was little or no violence.

But how could anyone be unaware of the way violence has moved from the home to the schools, from the bedroom into the halls and then the streets of our society? Where is this place where there is no domestic violence? And even if such a place existed, how could he ignore the news reports about battered women, the docudramas and plays and movies? How much do you have to see and read about before you "know" facts that provide a basis for inferential reasoning?

We are not machines and the brain is not a computer, at least not as far as I am concerned. It is too unpredictable and too quirky. I am not sure whether human beings have the ability to search as systematically as a computer would for counterexamples. But you don't need to have the precision of a machine to see the illogic of his position. If this young man is ignorant of violence done to women, of the brutality of domestic violence, his ignorance would have to be purposeful.[32]

I have had to conclude that much of what is expressed by white males in my classes these days is not reasoning at all but expressions of belief—blind faith, maintained in spite of all evidence to the contrary. Defiance of reason is the response of most white males to any challenge to their power, to their sense of entitlement.

If our discipline is a science, as Langdell would have us believe and as many argue we have forgotten, why is there no fidelity to truth? I am not asking for the truth of poetry, which might ask this student to see and know the suffering of both of the women in this case. I am asking for a narrower truth, the one governed by logic and reason, and a reality that can be established to the satisfaction of any scientist. But I am asking as a woman who happens to occupy the front of the room, and the resistance to the authority of women in the classroom is almost visceral. In young white men it comes from somewhere deep in their unconscious. And there is no responsibility taken for what they say. When challenged, they revert to a subjective test of intent, disclaiming knowledge of the shared meaning that forms the basis, in life or law, for our understanding of "objective" reality.

These students care nothing for the traditions of Karl Llewellyn or Arthur Corbin or the opinions of Benjamin Cardozo, the white males of the previous generation from whom I learned lessons about the law and logic and justice. My students employ economic models, the rhetoric of choice, assent, and efficiency; and their heroes are Richard Epstein and Richard Posner.

Thinking about Law and Economics, the Chicago school version in particular, always makes me tired, Louise. My attention has started to flag.

In spite of my excitement about the relevance of lectures delivered by Llewellyn to law students in 1929 to the contemporary discussion of cognitive science, I don't think I've made real progress. I haven't made a dent in the pile of readings Lee Knefelkamp left behind. Besides, sorting is pretty tedious. I'd like to go take a nap, anything other than lining these theories up and looking for similarities and differences.

Christopher and I used to have these battles about his toys and our very different strategies in cleaning his room. I would insist that every toy be returned to the box with like kind toys—G.I. Joes with G.I. Joes or with other superheroes, and Legos with Legos. And Chris thought the point was to get things off the floor. It didn't matter to him where the toys ended up. Of course, he could clean his room in a matter of minutes while I would spend hours sitting on the floor surrounded by different colored plastic shoe boxes in various sizes.

I am experiencing the same difficulty in the project of sorting bulbs. There are too many bulbs and I can't decide how much attention to detail I must pay in deciding where they go. Perhaps I am unsure of the taxonomies I should be using. It was easy enough sorting Masters of the Universe from G.I. Joes and Legos. It is easy enough to sort legal theories into their respective domains: contracts, torts, property, criminal law. But what criteria must I apply in sorting cognitive theories? Where to put each bulb? I am concerned that if I'm not careful the jonquils and the daffodils will end up together and the hyacinths and tulips will become all muddled.

Last year I got a little help from my friends. They helped me identify one source of my confusion. Kolb's discussion of cognitive theory and disciplinary difference introduced a different terminology. We were well along in the process of research and writing before I noticed that Perry referred to cognitive positions or stages while Kolb discussed cognitive styles. These terms are not synonymous.

My cousin, M'Lynn, who is an elementary school librarian, and two other good friends I have known since childhood, Carole and Mary, both of whom work with elementary school–age children, educated me on the difference between stages and styles in cognitive theory.

Mary, Carole, and I were sitting on a deck in upstate New York while Carole explained the meaning of cognitive style. "I could be packing to go to Alaska," she told me, "in the middle of the fall in New York. If it is Indian summer here and the temperature is eighty or ninety degrees, even though I know that it is much colder in Alaska—I have read the weather map and listened to the weather channel, I know they have had their first snowfall—when I get to Alaska, I will find that I have packed far too many lightweight clothes unsuitable for the weather there."

I think this is a wonderful story, one that illustrates the line of demarcation in cognitive theory between stages and styles. I want to use her example in this book, but Carole is somewhat hesitant. There is a negative value attached to what I perceive as a positive talent: her ability to perceive the world not just visually and aurally but also kinesthetically.

Now, I suppose I should explain at this point that I have

no doubt about where Carole fits in Perry's scheme. When Perry was struggling with those Harvard students, trying to move them out of Dualism, Carole had already left Dualism far behind. I have never had reason to doubt Carole's status as an intellectual or her ability to think critically. When we were in high school, she was reading Albert Camus and Jean-Paul Sartre and trying to explain the difference between existentialism and the theory of the absurd to me. I had about as much interest in French philosophers as I did in her other major passion, football, which she tried to teach me using clothespins she moved around the table.

Learning styles purport to explain the way we perceive or "know" information about the world and the way we process what we perceive. In Kolb's terms, Carole learns in ways that are both abstract and concrete. When she wants to know about French philosophy, she may read a book or listen to a lecture or watch a program on PBS. When she wants to know about the weather, she will read and listen and, whether she likes it or not, she will "feel" what the weather is. Her mind and her body are involved in the acquisition of knowledge about the weather. This contrast between the way she learns about existentialism and the way she learns about the weather also explains what Kolb means when he says that learning styles may vary depending on the knowledge or information one seeks to acquire.

This discussion of learning styles and the correlative teaching techniques assumes we have reached some sort of consensus about the "information" we want our students to acquire, and so will I. Let's assume that the MacCrate

Report has gained universal acceptance. We want our students to be problem solvers and we agree that for this they will need a cognitive tool kit. What is the proper instructional device for teaching a student to think like lawyers? Do different people with different learning styles learn to think in different ways?

You and I both teach large sections in the first year, Property and Contracts, respectively. We have been offered only two real possibilities as teaching techniques: the problem approach and the Socratic method. Of the two, the second has been the subject of the most criticism, including our own. We both share a concern with the way the Socratic method seems to invite sadism on the part of teachers. Don't underestimate the role of the student masochist.

There is something peculiarly male about the way some students, like the author of *Broken Contract*,[33] insist on a trial by ordeal. If they don't get it, they feel they have been cheated. Martha Minow was taken to task in *Broken Contract* for championing a new approach to law school education, an experiment designed to make Harvard Law School both more humane and more intelligible for law students. Richard Kahlenberg felt he was cheated because he was not taught Civil Procedure by Arthur Miller. The thing is, both Miller and Minow use the Socratic method. Apparently, Kahlenberg felt that she didn't use it to good effect. He was humbled, but not sufficiently humiliated.

It is sometimes hard to explain why I would choose a teaching method that has been so reviled, made to carry so much of the weight of the criticism of law school education. One answer might be that any approach that promises a dialogue between teacher and student appeals to me as a "couch and conversation" style teacher. But there is more to it than that. I suppose I actually believe that students can be taught how to reason through a problem if the Socratic method is used the right way.

Some who have observed me say that I am combative in the classroom. I prefer to think that I engage individual students in a discussion. Sometimes this slows the class down—brings it to a screeching halt, actually—as a student searches for an answer to my question. Other students get impatient; colleagues suggest techniques for "moving the class along." I don't understand the rush. Time is an important ingredient in problem solving—thinking time becomes a kind of breathing space, space that may be large enough for a very small garden.

By and large I have tried to stay away from the cognitive theorists in the field of experimental psychology or those who are enamored of information-processing models— those individuals who see the brain as computer. But one chapter in one book did capture my attention because it referred to reasoning with imperfect knowledge.[34] The authors invoked the Socratic dialogue as a means of teaching students how to gain knowledge through a process of inference. Questions like "why" or "why not" are supposed to force the student to think inductively, to draw inferences from the knowledge already there and available for use.

The authors apparently felt quite comfortable with the fact that a Socratic dialogue, in or out of law school, often feels like an inquisition. That danger is compounded in law school because law schools let a bunch of lawyers loose with a method of instruction that is inquisitorial. The student may be treated as if he or she is a hostile witness undergoing cross-examination. But what about those of us in law school teaching who were not trained to be litigators? The cognitive theorist authors offer another explanation for the discomfort of our students. Our students' pain is not so much a function of the way we ask questions as it is a consequence of their experience of ignorance.[35]

This teaching technique is painful for students who are unable to use—or who lack—the general knowledge which should be employed inferentially in answering a question. As one theorist put it, students who do not have general knowledge in an area often interpret questions that presume this kind of general knowledge as meaningless.[36] All the time and all the space in the world can't help this student.

Students should have the general knowledge they need to answer most questions in a first-year law class. Part of what we "know" for purposes of legal analysis is human behavior. We use that knowledge all the time in deciding what is reasonable, a favorite legal benchmark, or foreseeable, another standard invoked in different areas of the law.

The longer I teach, though, the more amazed I am at what appears to be a lack of general knowledge among our students. For a couple of years now, I have used cases involving givebacks by employees. I can't tell you how many students fail to see the loss experienced by the employees. They don't understand that the employees' relinquishment of a cost-of-living increase to which they are entitled is a benefit to the employer in the form of reduced costs. What they see is only what they are told—that the company didn't "really" benefit since it closed the factory anyway; that the employees did not experience any loss since they were able to work six months longer than they might have if they didn't agree to the rollback. Yet many of our students write in their applications to law school that they are the first person in their family to attend college or go to law school. They have parents who have worked and sacrificed to make sure that their children will have a better life. Is amnesia a prerequisite for upward mobility? Or are the very aspirations of their parents proof of the limited value of their labor if not their sacrifice?

From time to time I will force a student to defend a position he or she has taken. From time to time a student confronted with a question he can't answer will respond with his own question, "Why don't you tell me?" The printed page cannot communicate the tone in which this question is usually asked. Words are only an approximation here, but "snide" or "disrespectful" would be my first choice. I am also sure the students, mostly men, would say it was just a joke.

And if I do "tell" this student about the "facts" or the "truth" of the situation, his response would be that I have a particular political agenda and there can be no "truth" in anything I say. Maybe this is naïveté or Early Multiplicity; maybe it is the law school version of the lyrics from the 1970s, "There ain't no good guy. There ain't no bad guy. There's only you and me and we just disagree."[37]

Struggle as I will to convince them that there is a "truth" to be found, that there is a "right" way to reason through a problem, I don't seem to make much headway. I have devised ways to buttress my authority, knowing full well that anything that supports the facts I present to them will be immediately suspect. In Contracts, for instance, I show a film, a documentary using male and female "testers" in situations designed to show the biases that disadvantage women. In a variety of transactions—everything from dry cleaning shirts to getting a job—women were discriminated against.[38] I asked my students what this means. How can we build a theory of contracts around a model of value-maximizing behavior that is so flawed? How can we bargain for exchange when we start off on unequal footing? Who has more bargaining power, a man or a woman?

A student who has set himself up as my nemesis answers, "Women are clearly more powerful than men. Haven't you read Aristophanes' *Lysistrata?*"

While this allusion to the classics might please the Blooms and the Bennetts in our society, the advocates and defenders of the literary canon, I wondered whether the student understood on a conscious level what he had just done. If you asked this student what this statement meant to me, how it would be interpreted by a middle-aged, postmenopausal, overweight Black woman, he would disavow any intent to diminish my authority or to assert his superior power as a man. Quite the opposite. He had just acknowledged the powerlessness of men.

But I am not among those women who have the power to which he has referred and I certainly have no such power over him. There is no place in an intellectual universe that defines power in these terms for the facts that appear in the film I showed. We share the same perceptual apparatus, this student of mine and I, but he has eyes that do not see and ears that do not hear.

You see, Louise, whether we are discussing stages or styles, perception is the first step in learning. Understanding is the second step. If the Socratic method is hampered by the absence of shared "knowledge," a common perceptual basis for understanding and interpreting our existence, it is hard to see how the process will result in any real understanding. Analogical reasoning is too remote and too artificial for most students.

Part of my confusion about Kolb's piece and the idea of learning styles stemmed from the point of departure in the article. Kolb began with Piaget and the theory that we move from phenomenolistic (concrete) to constructivist (abstract) and from egocentric (active) to a reflective (internalized) way of knowing. By now, even I know Piaget is a signal that we must be talking about development, and to me that means stages. But Kolb then introduces a whole new vocabulary to describe what may be biologically determined preferences with respect to learning. People, or rather learners, fall into different categories: divergers, convergers, assimilators and accommodators.[39] And these categories can be superimposed on the graph he constructed. Concrete/active (first quadrant) learners are accommodators. Reflective/concrete (second quadrant) learners are divergers. Abstract/active learners are convergers, and abstract/reflective learners are assimilators.

This all begins to sound familiar, and I realize I am back to those initials, the typology Chris couldn't remember when he set up his opposition between formal learners and informal learners. Chris was typed using a Murphy-Meisgeier test, in which the learning styles were labeled introversion, intuition, sensing, and perceiving. Recently a similar typing device, the Myers-Briggs test, has been promoted as a means for lawyers to "learn more about themselves and to understand the differences between themselves and others."[40] It is said to describe the test taker's cognitive preferences.

According to this typology, lawyers tend toward introversion. They prefer to consider all the facts before answering to leave time for internal processing. Lawyers need to understand a situation or a concept before experiencing it.

Lawyers are also typed as either sensing or intuitive. I think these two sound the same, but sensing means the person is something of an empiricist. He or she learns by observation and experience. The intuitive person, on the other hand, prefers open-ended problems that need creative solutions.

They say most lawyers are thinkers, meaning that they are logical and objective. They solve problems by collecting, organizing, and evaluating data, but they also need to know the critiera that are used to judge them and they need recognition for their achievements. They want to know cause and effect.

And finally, most lawyers are judgers. They want a routine followed consistently; they want to know exactly what is expected of them; they value clarity and consistency. Excuse me, Louise, but weren't these the habits of mind that were so much disparaged by Perry and Bloom? Some of them sound to me so much like Dualism it's embarrassing.

The Myers-Briggs typology is a hodgepodge of psychoanalytic jargon, Jungian in its feel, that has some loose connection to cognitive preferences. There is an even more elaborate and sophisticated version, which is probably more relevant to our inquiry: Canfield's Learning Styles Inventory.[41] This theory has nine categories—can you believe it? The nine learner typologies are social, independent, applied, conceptual, social/applied, social/conceptual, independent/applied, independent/conceptual, and neutral preference. To figure out where a student belongs, the tester has to determine the student's preferred mode of learning: listening, reading, iconic, or direct experience.

Finally, I feel we are getting someplace. At least this final list includes what seems like relevant information, something that describes instructional techniques, that refers explicitly to the "basic sensory and cognitive modality in which new information may be acquired."[42] Translation: some people acquire knowledge using words, others are more visual. An iconic learner, for instance, prefers graphs or pictorial representation. "The iconic scale includes all types of non word media such as videotapes, movies, charts, graphs, displays, slides, blackboard and flip chart details. Persons indicating a strong preference for iconics are expressing a need to see concepts in forms where interrelationships and visual expressions other than language are used."[43]

If there is one thing we have noticed about our students, it is their lack of interest in the printed word and their greater reliance on alternative means of learning. Suppose these are not the alternative modes of learning anymore, but the dominant modes? The problem may not be our students but our own ignorance of the way teaching and learning have been transformed by technological advances. Perception is only the first step in learning. Understanding is the second step. For some, the only way to make something their own is to act on it. According to learning style theorists, some people learn by trying out a new theory, and others learn through a process called "reflection." They like to think about it and turn it over in their minds before they use their new knowledge.

Before we began this journey, Louise, if anyone had asked me where either of us belonged in the graph that maps Kolb's learning universe, I would have placed you in the abstract/reflective quadrant and me in the one labeled concrete/applied. I would have labeled you independent/ conceptual using Canfield's typology. You are, after all, the person who will not switch from WordPerfect to Word because you say you don't have the time to learn it. When forced to use my computer, you write down the instructions in elaborate detail, while I am perfectly comfortable learning through a process of trial and error, figuring out the glyphs and the commands when I need them.

Yet when it came to Perry's scheme, you plunged ahead while I lagged behind, muttering to myself and gathering material around me. You designed and executed a project while I continued to read, parsing through the theories to construct some kind of framework that would allow me to act. I was suspicious of Perry's scheme. Lee Knefelkamp's lecture and our problem-solving sessions had not answered my questions. I could not form a plan until I understood why women and students of color begin at stage 3 in the Perry scheme, but their success in academic institutions is not commensurate with their elevated status in this hierarchy. I could not implement a plan that was descriptive but not necessarily explanatory.

Kolb may have an explanation for the role reversal I have noted. It is his description of the final stage of cognitive development or a mature learner's cognitive style: Integration. Apparently, once you are no longer a student, the learning styles that are preferred in your discipline cease to have the same power. Kolb concludes that once students leave the institution of higher education, they enter a stage of "adult development" where "the highest states of development are characterized by personal integrations of complex, highly articulated views of the world and one's experience of it. From the perspective of experiential learning theory, this goal is attained through a dialectical process of adaptation, achieved through the expression of nondominant modes of dealing with the world and their higher level integration with specialized functions."[44] Someone else calls this "pragmatic intelligence" or wisdom.[45] Most of our adult life is spent using practical knowledge rather than academic knowledge.

Once again Kolb uses a diagram, in this case one that is

supposed to depict the dialectical process that is an experiential learning model. I think it looks more like the life cycle of learning or an intellectual Ferris wheel.

Learning moves clockwise:

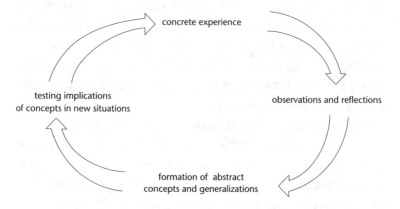

I suppose the dialectical part is the description of the model as "an interactive process where . . . experience and knowledge are repeatedly transformed."[46] If I had to describe the difference between our approaches in terms of this model, I would say you have made it full circle while I am stuck down at the bottom of this Ferris wheel wondering whether the motor put-putting and wheezing beside me is strong enough to get me up to the top and back down again.

The good news, Louise, is that when I leave this carnival of cognitive theories, I will have almost finished my autumnal task. I am left with two bulbs and I can't decide what to do with them. I can't quite decide whether Kolb's description of cognitive styles and cognitive preferences belongs with the Perry bulbs. Do you think this is a tulip bulb or does it look more like a dahlia?

At first glance, probably because they both refer to a dialectical process, I thought Integration was merely another way of describing Commitment. I tried to create a chart with Perry's stages and Kolb's styles lined up side by side the way I did with Perry's stages and critical thinking's list of skills. Try as I might, I could not see any real parallel between the two, other than the determined attempt by both to develop schemes that accommodate difference within an established hierarchy. Perry employs the metaphor of a Pilgrim's Progress.[47] In Kolb there is less of the uncertain and indefinable blurring of the moral and intellectual development.

I have uncovered another reason why I find Perry's scheme vaguely unsettling. He resolves epistemological and ethical questions with a sort of reduction: the simple transformation of a lowercase c to an uppercase C as the learner moves from commitment born of indifference and ignorance to Commitment that is the agency for self-actualization. Perry ignores those who say that intellectual development and moral development are very different things; he blends the two kinds of development, locating intellectual approaches on a moral continuum.

To be truthful, there is nothing in the idea of combining moral and intellectual development that offends me. Quite the opposite. What does disturb me is the sense of self in this model that posits some sort of "universal" identity. This universal identity transcends a sense of community built on "tribal, racial, class or ideological boundaries."[48] Here now, what does this mean? What is the cost? Must we abandon the other communities in our lives for one based on our "shared realization of aloneness"?[49] Who would accept that kind of invitation?

Perry has created a link between intellectual and moral development using dialectical reasoning.[50] He uses a quote to distinguish Commitment from the inflexibility of Dualism. Commitment is a vision of "provisional ultimacy: remembering its inadequacy and open to new truth but also committed to the absoluteness of the truth which it inadequately comprehends and expresses."[51] Why does this quote talk about "it" as though the vision had some life of its own, acting of its own volition instead of being acted on by those who share the vision?

Howard Gardner provides an alternative to Perry's universality. Gardner invites us into the domain of metacognition. Instead of classifying the artist as someone who has experienced "regression in service of the ego,"[52] reconciling the value embedded in the hierarchy of intelligence with the conflicting value placed on certain nonanalytical human activities, Howard Gardner talks about different kinds of intelligence.[53]

It is not hard to wrap your mind around this theory, to appreciate the idea of different intelligences and the escape it provides from the tyranny of intelligence as a monolithic presence in our lives. It is easy for me to accept the idea that what I know is directly related to my ability to think in a particular way *and* it is a relief to know that we don't all have to be measured by the same yardstick.

I am free to admit that I don't see or understand spatial relationships.[54] I never made the transition from advanced algebra, in which I was extremely competent, to solid geometry. In solid geometry I was introduced to that mathematical conundrum, the sphere. I never could solve problems; I could only memorize those theorems they told me I needed to know. My math teacher did not chide; he merely noted that I was "stuck in flatland." Years later, I read that "Thinking in three dimensions is like learning a foreign language."[55] I am good with languages, but space is a language I have never learned.

The geography of my mind presents certain practical problems for me. For instance, I have never been very good at parallel parking. It is easier for me to back into a space than to turn into it. I can parallel park on the right side of the road, but not on the left. Similarly, I have never been good with Tupperware, the plastic containers that come in so many different shapes and sizes, the homemaker's best friend. I can never manage to guess the size of the container needed to store leftovers. I start to pour spaghetti sauce, for instance, into one of the plastic bowls and find that the bowl is filled and there is still sauce in the pan. My friend Cheryl, however, could tell immediately whether the container was the right size. She understood the idea of volume.

On the other hand, in another area of perception, I am, my dentist Dr. Robert Sachs insists, particularly sensitive. Pain, he says, is a matter of perception. It is entirely subjective, which is not the same as saying that it is not real. Some people feel no pain at all even when the thickest, pulpiest nerves are touched. And some people are even more sensitive than I am. No amount of Novocain works on them. They feel everything. Dr. Sachs cites an example of the opposite, the lucky individuals who can lie on nails. I challenge his classificatory scheme and point out that these are people who work at entering an altered state of consciousness. "Precisely my point," he says as he sticks the needle into my jaw, "it is all a matter of perception."

Robert Sachs doesn't know it, but he has just offered me a metaphor that I accept graciously. It is the perception of pain that separates me from many of my students. I feel the pain of social injustice. I see the law as a means of remedying injustice. My students appear to be numb—stoicism with the help of an emotional anesthetic. The psychological equivalent of Novocain is fatalism, an attribute of contemporary American culture introduced by means of the rhetoric of scarcity. These students believe themselves and the law to be powerless.

Perception is what this entire project is all about, perception and understanding. When I sit back and look at the assortment of ideas that have been displayed before us, I know I have to make some choices. I accept the idea that some forms of intelligence are indispensable to our discipline, but I also believe that we may not fully appreciate the role multiple intelligences play in this profession. Don't you think a patent attorney with no spatial intelligence would be at a distinct disadvantage?

I agree that we have to be concerned with the meaning our students assign to learning, but we also have to think critically about the meaning assigned by the educational institution and the people who teach in it. Have we legitimated the idea of a single measure of intelligence by placing far too much weight on a single test score, the LSAT? How can this one test measure the one thing a good lawyer needs above all else, practical intelligence or common sense?[56]

We need to think about what we teach in a very different way. The cognitive skills that are critical to success in law school may actually become less important in the practice of law. Practice and problem solving may require a wider variety of cognitive skills and maybe even the application of different forms of intelligence.

We need to consider whether wisdom can be taught. Wisdom may begin with an acknowledgment that intellectual development cannot be severed from experience or moral development. And finally, when we have sorted through all the psychological jargon and the complex typologies, we have to acknowledge that there are different ways to acquire information. When it comes to learning styles, when it comes to the matter of how we communicate information to our students, the trip from Dualism to Commitment can be made by means of any perceptual apparatus, visual, aural, or even kinesthetic.

I have finally sorted it all out, Louise, and I know what I have to work with. I can plan my garden now that I know the different varieties and the quantity of each kind of bulb. I can begin to imagine the spring, from the moment the first crocus pokes out from under the snow, followed almost immediately by the wild abandon of grape hyacinths, the sedate and understated beauty of jonquils and the brighter and more cheerful daffodils to the final, most spectacular of the spring flowers, the tulips. The sequence is important, but so are location and light and color and texture. I am guided by my own sense of artistry in deciding what arrangement will allow the most flowers to bloom and make my garden beautiful.

Winter

SITTING
AROUND
THE
FIRE

SEVEN

Winter

❄

PRIVACY
AND
THE
PARKING
LOT
FACES

The dead of winter is an introspective season. The holidays
are over, and white has ceased to be a wonder. The nights
are long, the mornings dark. Spring is just an idea; there is
no smell of it in the air, and I am stuck with myself for
company.

I have been thinking about our project on cognitive
theory, Deborah—about how and why our colleagues re-
sisted it. I have also been thinking about our recent dis-

agreement on the nature of peer review. Our stances on how to judge effective teaching are predictable: you enter the arena fearlessly, armed with your glorious anger, keen political sense, and moral certainty. I am sitting on a sagging bench, with a blanket wrapped around my shoulders and pulled over my head like a monk's caul, worried about survival—yours and mine. You see challenge, I see risk. My thoughts are about law teaching and privacy.

It is not just true of law teaching: all work has its public and private dimensions, and only the person inside the work knows which is which. Someone outside the work might try to draw the line, choosing some external boundary to designate the public and private aspects of the job. Before I went to law school, Deborah, while you were in graduate school, I was a salesclerk for five years in Austin, Texas, first at Gem Fabrics, and later and much longer at London Fabrics. As in most stores, there was work on the floor and work in the storeroom. At London's, a heavy yellow curtain separated the two areas. Someone outside my work would have speculated that the cleavage between its public and private spheres approximated the yellow curtain. A reasonable speculation, but anyone with a history in retail sales knows that it's dead wrong.

In the storeroom, where goods and people were stacked in a very deliberate way, there was hierarchy—the suffocating proximity of the manager and the managed, the intimacy of the overworked and underpaid, the coffee break out in the open, under fluorescent scrutiny, the unwritten code of the right way to be. There were no whispers or secrets, not even conversations, since every word spoken in a storeroom is universally owned. All statements became announcements by virtue of having hit the air.

In the breakroom, silence was forbidden. I could not read books at lunch because it was deemed subversive and antisocial. Daydreaming signaled a possible drug abuse problem. What you wore and who drove you to work, what you said and did not say, how much you earned an hour, how much commission you made, what you paid for rent, and when you arrived on the planet were all subject to collective inference. There was no privacy.

But on the floor, where the magic of selling was performed, each salesclerk was on her own. There was no direct supervision, no correct way to roam the aisles of fabric, no manual for greeting a customer, no script for exchanging information about a dress, a window, or a Christmas tree skirt. There was no sanction for doing things differently, only the absolute freedom of the bottom line: how much fabric did you sell today?

In this very public space, privacy was permitted. Amidst the forests of chintz and moiré satin, in the canyons of rickrack and lace, adrift on a sea of velvet of every imaginable hue, I daydreamed and wrote poetry. I smiled and talked and laughed, all on automatic pilot, always engaged in an inner dialogue, often of darkness and despair, but mine and mine alone. And every week, when the commissions were tallied, I earned myself another week of privacy on the floor. In many ways, it was a creative job, helping others take something flat like fabric and turn it into dresses, curtains, slipcovers, costumes, and crafts—something useful and three-dimensional. I loved those fabrics, the way they felt to the touch, their rich colors, their smell, their shivering submission to stainless steel. And in my own chatty way, and mute misery, I made Ed London a lot of money.

Now I sing for my supper. I teach and I write. And just as an outsider might err about where things fall on either side of the yellow curtain at London Fabrics, so might he misjudge the line between the public and private dimensions of law school teaching. He might speculate that the teaching is the public part and the writing the private. Once again, it would be a reasonable speculation. After all, when I teach law, it is usually in a large room shaped like an amphitheater which seats no fewer than a hundred people, who stare at me and copy down what I say. For a few seconds before class, in the school's bathroom, I check out my hair, and sigh at my mother's middle-aged faced peering out at me from the mirror. And of course, when I teach, I usually wear the armor of work clothes, as my father used to say.

My father ran a small water well business in central Ohio, and he did not wear suits to work. However, when he had a business meeting to attend, he would announce to the family at the dinner table that he would have to wear his "armor" in the morning. In a business suit, he told me, he always felt more protected and less like a "soft-shelled crab." The suit performed another important function: it sent the message to the waitress that you were to be seated at the table with the other men in suits. It was important in business, he used to say, to sit at the right table.

During the Middle Ages, both men and their horses wore armor corresponding to the ancient German designation of offensive and defensive weapons. Offensive weapons included "various missiles, cutting and thrusting instruments, bows, cross-bows, javelins, lances, partisans, mallets, clubs, battle-axes, and so on. The other included helmets, coats of mail, sheathings for the arms and legs, gauntlets, hauberks, shields, and horse-armour."[1] My father was a shy man, and terrible at business. His armor was defensive. A meeting made him feel besieged, as indeed he was, and he felt that his business suit protected him from the missiles and mallets of aggression. They were clothes for the public arena, just like my teaching clothes. And like my father, I wear them defensively, to give me wider shoulders, to hide and protect my female body, to ward off cutting and thrusting instruments, to sheathe and shield, and ultimately to be seated at the right table.

But when I write, I wear sweatpants and my grey sweater. I pull my hair straight back in a pony tail, and I wear no face at all, neither my own nor my mother's; I am not burdened by reflection. It is dark, and I am alone, and there is usually a cat on my lap. I never teach with a cat on my lap, although I would like to. Writing looks like a private activity.

Here the outsider's speculation about the private and public aspects of this work is not dead wrong. It is just too black and white. While there are many indicia of privacy in the process of writing, namely, solitude and silence, if the words come from the heart, privacy is lost. I am always accompanied by ghosts when I write—absent loved ones and ancient enemies, grandchildren who are not yet born, the judgmental, brown-eyed girl I used to be. And writing that matters to me is almost always revelatory, regardless of whether the narrator is real or fictional. The reader is granted access to the inner life of another person, and the boundary between self and other becomes blurred. That blurring, for me, is the primary motivation for reading, and in some mysterious way, for writing—relief from the loneliness of being me. So despite the seclusion, and the cat, the act of writing ends up being the publication of the private.

Perhaps more surprising, though, is the private nature of the classroom, at least from the teacher's point of view. We assume that teaching is public since it takes place in such a theatrical setting. And from the student's point of view, the classroom can be the most public of arenas. I remember it well, the sitting-down perspective of my first year at Texas, those Formica desks and polyurethane screwed-to-the-floor swivel chairs, the locus of a lot of sweating palms and acute anxiety. But for the teacher, there is a feeling of privacy about a classroom. Once the door is closed, only those inside know what goes on. In the parlance of trusts and estates, it is a closed class, a hermetically sealed universe; no new hearts and minds can enter the classroom. Not only that, those who inhabit the room with you cannot tell you what to do. The privacy for the teacher stems from the freedom to choose the form and substance of the class, and also from the lack of peer scrutiny and control. The lack of privacy for the student stems from the loss of control, and from the intense scrutiny of one's peers and one's superior.

Of course, it is a dictatorship. The teacher has all the power, the student none. The teacher picks the book, charts the course, determines how the class will be run, makes the assignments, monopolizes the podium unless he chooses to yield it to another, sets the criteria and assesses whether the student has met them, an assessment from which there is no appeal. The student's only recourse against a tyrant is to exit the course or refuse to enter it in the first place, although with required courses and limited offerings, even these options are often foreclosed.

We treat the classroom much as we treat the family. Absent evidence of abuse and neglect, we turn our eyes from our neighbors' windows. Parental power is wielded within the walls of our homes without supervision or intervention—almost without limitation. Students in a classroom and children in a family are in the same situation: vulnerable and (because what is done to them goes unwitnessed) unprotected—all in the name of privacy. Indeed, the privacy is a necessary condition for the exercise of this power, and any invasion, any breaking of the castle's close, will not be welcomed by its keeper.

Just as it does with families, the state imposes limits on what can take place in a classroom. Various forms of verbal abuse will not be tolerated. At Indiana State University, for example, there was a math professor who read Bible verses aloud to his math students for several minutes at the beginning of each class hour; students who did not want to listen were "free" to leave the classroom.[2] After receiving several warnings that the readings were contrary to university policy, and after advising the university that he was going to continue the practice, the professor was dismissed. The court upheld the dismissal on the grounds that his readings violated the students' constitutional rights. The court expressly recognized the coercive power that I am talking about. Regarding the opportunity to step into the hallway, the court responded, "Peer pressure, fear of the teacher, concern about grades, and the alternative of standing outside the classroom in the hall, severely limit the freedom of the student to absent himself from class during a Bible reading."[3] While the state had not directly participated in the professor's readings, "it placed him in the position of authority from which he might express his religious views during a part of the curricular day, involving young people whose presence is compelled by law, hence utilizing the prestige, power, and influence of school authority."[4]

There are limits too on the use of profanity. At least one case in higher education, *Martin v. Parrish,* upheld the termination of an economics instructor due to his inveterate use of profane language, including, "hell," "God damn," "bullshit," and such phrases as "The attitude of this class sucks" and "If you don't like the way I teach this God damn course there is the door."[5] One student called his castigation of the class "an explosion, an unprovoked, extremely offensive, downgrading of the entire class."[6] The professor sued under Section 1983, alleging a deprivation of his First Amendment right of free speech, abridgment of academic freedom, and denial of due process and equal protection. The court affirmed the district court's judgment for the college, viewing "the role of higher education as no less pivotal to our national interest [than high school education]. It carries on the process of instilling in our citizens necessary democratic virtues, among which are civility and moderation. It is necessary to the nurture of knowledge and resourcefulness that undergird our economic and political system."[7]

Personally, I have known of a few law teachers who have verbally abused their students in this very same fashion, and I am not so confident that the state would step in. In a concurring opinion to *Martin,* Judge Hill expressed his concern that the majority did not give sufficient weight to the differences between high school settings and college classrooms. High school instruction should be more structured in order to "teach basic social, moral and political values," whereas college education should be more of a "free-wheeling experience," in order to force "students to analyze their basic beliefs."[8] I can only assume that Judge Hill would consider graduate education—including, perhaps, law school—to be the most freewheeling educational environment of them all, and hence deserving of less protection. He would be wrong about the law school, however, particularly in the first year.

There is a process of infantilization during the first year of law school that is the direct result of our poor pedagogy. Like a child trying to figure out the lay of the land, a first-year student is purposely kept in the dark. As one student put it, "In law school, professors expected students to memorize the professor-made lists, but the lists were with-held—students were supposed to guess what was on the lists before they memorized them. . . . Law school was like coming into a movie when it was half over."[9] Our failure to treat the student as an adult by revealing the rules of the game makes children of them, at least for a period of time. I have come into the women's bathroom at our school on a number of occasions and seen grown women sobbing uncontrollably at a professor's verbal attacks and profanity. I would like to think there was some way to stop the invective, but I suspect Judge Hill is right: the further up the ladder you go, the greater the scope of academic freedom. Freedom to bully and abuse.

Exploring the analogy of classroom to family, there must be forms of pedagogical neglect as well, but I only found one case on the subject that even arguably applied. In *Carley v. Arizona Board of Regents,* a university art teacher in his fifth year of teaching challenged his nonretention, charging that his teaching methods were constitutionally protected speech.[10] He frequently left "his classes unat-tended during appointed meeting times in order to teach students to be more self-reliant. He further describes his methods as emphasizing independent student work in or-der to reflect the expectations which students will encoun-ter in the business world."[11] The original committee vote from the art department was only three to two against retention, and the teacher had the support of his dean. Not only that, the university's Academic Freedom and Tenure Committee found by a six to three vote that his rights to academic freedom had been violated. Still, the university administration voted for nonretention, and the court upheld its decision. The *Carley* case provides a glimpse into academic politics, an instance where the teacher's conduct seems not to have violated the norms of the art department, or even the larger community of university professors, but offended the central administration. It is hard for me to imagine a law school putting up with a teaching method such as not showing up for class. A law teacher found guilty of pedagogical neglect would probably go to a lower circle of hell than one found guilty of pedagogical abuse. Indeed, I suspect the latter crime would go unprosecuted.

Personally, I have come to hate the power I wield in the privacy of my classroom, which is why I would rather sell fabric than teach law. If only there were some ideas woven into the warp and woof of retail sales—Chinese fortune cookies with thought-provoking messages hidden in the bolts, tucked between the folds of fabric, to be stumbled upon when straightening the stacks on a rainy, customerless day. If only there were poetry printed randomly on the selvages. If only selling fabric did not pay minimum wage. If only I did not care what people think of me.

It is this aspect of privacy in the classroom, and caring what people think of us that made our project so difficult, Deborah. When we first got the idea of educating ourselves and our colleagues about cognitive theory, we naively assumed that everyone would think it was a good idea. In truth, many of our colleagues did think it was, but a surprising number did not.

They complained about the volume and difficulty of the

readings, though few seemed to have read them before or after the retreat. (Odd, isn't it, that a group of stellar former students should now make such indifferent ones? Did it make a difference that no one was getting a grade?) We made several formal, and many informal, invitations to our colleagues to engage in a journaling project with us, to experiment with some aspect of the newly acquired cognitive theory in their courses, to respond to questionnaires sent out before and after the retreat. Except for a few predictably adventurous souls, our invitations fell on deaf ears. While almost everyone was charmed by Lee Knefelkamp at the retreat, and most were intrigued by what she had to say about the stages of cognitive development, I don't think many of our colleagues took her message to heart.

I have wondered for some time why this was so, whether the failure to engage colleagues was our fault, Deborah, or whether there is something about our law school that made such a project flop. In a sweeping gesture of exculpation, I have decided that you and I were not the problem, and that our law school is probably a better place than most to try such a project out. Granted, we are on the fringe of the faculty, but it would be presumptuous, possibly paranoid, to assume that our identity had much to do with the lack of response. Anyone making such an invitation could and probably would be ignored. Similarly, our faculty does value teaching, and we got enthusiastic institutional support. As usual, our dean had nothing but green lights working in his traffic signal.

So why was Lee Knefelkamp's message so hard to take to

heart? It was such a simple one: an exhortation to assess and communicate. All she recommended was that we look at our courses to determine what kinds of cognitive tasks were involved and that we notify our students of the quality and quantity of intellectual effort required for the course.

It was such a simple message, but hard advice to take. Lee Knefelkamp assumed we all knew what kind of thought our courses required, but I, for one, did not, something I am chagrined to admit after almost ten years of teaching. Indeed, the assessment of the kinds of cognitive tasks needed to survive my Property course was painful. I came to realize that memorization of a great deal of messy doctrine was necessary. It made me feel so lowly, so Gilbertish—like one of those commercial outlines of black letter law our students surreptitiously buy and keep in their lockers. Knefelkamp also assumed that there would be some upper-level thought in all our courses, some sort of overarching theory. This I had little difficulty locating in Property, but I was embarrassed at what a hodgepodge of jurisprudential junk it was. It continues to be a crazy quilt of ideas, and I am still working to position them into a unifying rectangular border. It is tedious and sometimes discouraging work—work that forces me to confront my inadequacy.

But I am a puritan, Deborah, and confronting my inadequacy comes naturally to me. Sometimes I think I belong to the wrong century. I should have been a seventeenth-century Puritan, eking out an existence in the new world. The Puritans abhorred ostentation, refrained from personal amusement, and emphasized "industry and piety."[12] No one was allowed to outwardly manifest pride, and pride was publicly censured. One man's application for church membership was deferred "because of his self-confidence, and elsewhere members were censured for the pride of 'inordinate walking.' "[13] (As you well know, Deborah, that is one of my crimes: inordinate walking.) My attitudes toward "time management" are also distinctly Puritan. Cotton Mather, in extolling the virtues of his deceased brother, Nathanael, wrote in 1710 that Nathanael "apprehended that the idle minutes of our lives were many more than a short liver should allow: that the very filings of gold, and of time, were exceeding precious; and, that there were little fragments of hours intervening between our more stated business, wherein our thoughts of God might be less pleasant than frequent with us."[14] One writer characterized this habit of using idle moments as redeeming time.[15]

I love to redeem time; it is my art form. You have even suggested, Deborah, that my attitude toward time has an effect on my cognitive style, and I am sure you are right. You also always sound so sad for me when we discuss my puritan work ethic, and that frustrates me. Living inside it the way I do, I actually derive great joy from my work, and perform it with passion. And I know you don't believe it, but I don't think you—or anyone else for that matter— should become a puritan. It is the worst thing about being a puritan in the late twentieth century: you make other people uncomfortable. The mindset of other people is actually more seventeenth-century than mine because they assume that industry, piety, and time redemption are mandated. I want no one to model themselves after me, only to be responsible, and that can be achieved in a variety of ways.

I have been thinking about my puritanism, and my relations with colleagues, and the advice that Lee Knefelkamp gave us at the retreat. She wanted us to look closely at our courses and our teaching, and that is what I chose to do. And as a puritan, I regard this kind of spackling and sandpapering of the self, this preparation of the surface for a new coat of paint, as a necessary part of growth and redemption. But if the consummate, pain-in-the-ass puritan on the faculty was feeling undue agony and embarrassment at taking Lee Knefelkamp's message to heart, what about her colleagues of a less puritanical persuasion?

What about those who learned to cover the surface of a wall from the superintendent of their grandmother's rent-controlled apartment? How much fun could the application of cognitive theory be for them? What would their response be upon discovering that their overarching theory was a disorderly pile of blocks, or worse yet, that there were no blocks at all? Lee Knefelkamp was asking a lot of us, to take a long hard look at the wall, to take inventory not only of our students and our courses, but more dangerously, of ourselves. This was not a woman to fill in a crevice with extra paint, or to cover a cockroach with the casual stroke of a brush.

There were other barriers to taking her advice. Her incitation to communicate the cognitive tasks required for the course poses a threat to the teacher's tremendous power in the classroom. A teacher who puts students on notice of the kind of intellectual effort needed to survive a course yields a lot of mystery. Furthermore, such a communication alleviates the students' fears and anxieties, and I am not certain this is a desideratum among all our faculty. There are more than a few, I suspect, who want their students to remain fearful and anxious because it enhances the teacher's authority.

Personal exposure and the undermining of professorial authority are the obvious dangers in taking Lee Knefelkamp's advice. I see another danger, however, insidious and indirect, and given our disagreement about peer review, it is probably not something that you, Deborah, would classify as such. I am afraid that Lee Knefelkamp's advice poses an implicit threat to the teacher's academic freedom. What would Promotion and Tenure Committee meetings be like if we were to adopt her suggestions as a norm? What would we discuss in our assessment of a candidate's teaching ability if he were actually required to articulate his cognitive goals for each course? I am fairly certain that the level of discussion would be elevated, and that we might be able to dispense with the petty battle over how to characterize those casual, deadly deposits that angry students sometimes make in their teacher evaluations. We would have something substantive to talk about: a teacher's aspirations and whether he had met them.

But therein lies the rub. There would be two things to talk about: the dream and whether the dream has come true. About the desirability of assessing the worth of the dream, Deborah, you and I will part company. I am acutely uncomfortable passing judgment on a colleague's teaching goals, and you are not. This comes down, as always, to our very different philosophical bents, to my skepticism and belief in a pragmatic notion of truth, and to your faith in an ultimate truth and morality.

Remember our argument over how you behaved in a grocery line? You and Christopher were standing in line behind your cart, reading magazines, when a parent in front of you disciplined a young child with a slap on the face. You said something to the parent, expressing your disapproval, and she turned her abuse from the child to you. You had a loud, public exchange, not so much about the propriety of her slap as about the propriety of your intervention. When you got out to the parking lot, your son expressed mortification over your "butting into somebody else's business." I didn't give much credence to his response because of his adolescent predisposition to criticize all maternal action. Still, much to your dismay, when you asked me what I thought about your behavior, I had to side with Christopher. While I would never slap my own child's face, at home or in public, neither would I have said anything to the parent in the grocery store.

My silence may derive partly from timidity, from loathing confrontation of any kind. But it also derives from a respect for my vast ignorance about the other shopper's situation. She may be a good parent in many other ways; she may love her child fiercely, but be under terrible pressures—too little money, too little sleep, too little opportunity. She may even be demented from motherhood. I do not know what drives her to slap her child. Mill uses this argument to support his harm principle,[16] that we must let competent adults decide how to behave for themselves since they alone inhabit the situation and have the best means to know all the facts relevant to a decision.[17] You would counter, I anticipate, that the harm principle permits intervention if the behavior harms another person, here the weeping child in the grocery cart. Then I would argue that we don't know what benefits that mother may bestow upon him to outweigh the slap, or whether the slap is worse than telling a child he is stupid. And we would argue, as everyone who has read *On Liberty* does, about what kind of harm Mill means, but the bottom line is that you and I would still behave differently in the grocery store.

At least in certain arenas of life, you are certain there is a right and wrong way to behave, whereas I am committed to my state of uncertainty. Mind you, I am not talking about whether there could ever be a justification for Hitler's behavior, but whether under certain circumstances, a parental slap might be morally forgivable, or at least ignorable by the next person in the grocery line.

And in the context of evaluating pedagogical goals, I am only certain of one thing, that you will be certain, and I will not. Whether we are talking about how to behave in the grocery line or how to approach the assessment of a colleague's teaching, the structure of our argument remains the same. You are going to hold passionate ideas about the ultimate purposes of law teaching, and I am going to infuriate you by not sharing your passion.

What would happen, for example, if one of our colleagues stated the following as his sole pedagogical goal: to impart to my students the important doctrines of contract law. What if there were no mention of any loftier aspirations such as the transmission of moral values, or the inculcation of professional ethics, or an exploration of the jurisprudence of what makes a promise stick? All that was promised, to be delivered via the traditional case method, was the body of contract law, an understanding of Article 2 of the U.C.C., and some history, since it is virtually impossible to make sense of the law without understanding where it came from. While I might not want to take such a course with this colleague, I am willing to accept that he might be a competent, thorough, and boring teacher of contract law.

What's more, I think there is room in our law school for some competent, thorough, and boring teachers. After all, many of our students are going to become competent, thorough, and boring lawyers, and they need role models too. The more elite institutions may be able to fill their faculty slots with stellar lights, but at our school, I am willing from time to time to put up with less wattage, as long as the teacher is knowledgeable about the substantive law, intelligent, and prepared.

Several of our colleagues to whom this description might apply also make valuable contributions elsewhere in the institution. They may not be stars in the classroom, but they coach moot court teams, supervise student-edited journals, write self-studies, admit the entering class, organize symposia. When do we stop being teachers? At Harvard, the answer was clear: as soon as the lecture was over. The teachers at Harvard Law School all seemed to have one switch: on and off. Many were brilliant in the classroom, but once they left the podium they never spoke to students, never read or commented on papers, never bothered to find out about their students' intellectual interests or their lives in and out of law school. I felt so unimportant and invisible the year I was a student at Harvard. At least at Texas, there were doors with professors behind them once I learned how to knock. Thinking back on it now, I suppose some of the faces behind those doors belonged to competent, thorough, and boring teachers, but that is not how I remember them. I remember them as wonderful people who were interested in me.

And so I worry about these colleagues. If we set up a system of peer review that requires us to evaluate each other's cognitive goals and methods of achieving them, wonderful people might get the ax. It's bad enough that we sit in judgment on each other's scholarship; that already gives us ample space for pomposity and hidden political agendas. But what is the Promotion and Tenure Committee going to say to this competent, thorough, and boring teacher if it is unhappy with his stated cognitive goals? Get some ideas, or you will lose your job? That is like asking someone to shorten his nose, and is almost guaranteed to result in the generation of bad ideas, just as the requirement that everyone be a scholar results in the generation of bad articles.

Besides, what would happen if the dominant culture in the law school were made up of competent, thorough, and boring teachers? Imagine if certain members of our faculty were multiplied severalfold and given political power on the Promotion and Tenure Committee. One of them might observe your critical race theory approach to contracts, or my historical musings on Spencer's case, and say get rid of those ideas, or you will lose your job. I value the length of my nose too much, I suppose, and worry about the integrity of your face. You are much more open than I am, and therefore court amputation. I have learned to hide my ideas behind humor and self-deprecation. It would be all well and good, Deborah, to talk about setting standards for the teaching of law, as long as you and I, or other like-minded people, get to choose the standards, or the standard setters.

Remember what happened to Derrick Bell at Stanford Law School? He employed some nontraditional teaching methods in his Constitutional Law class, including introducing a racial perspective.[18] Without consulting Bell, a few faculty members, with some degree of approval from the administration, organized some enrichment lectures, intending to supplement coverage of the Con Law course. Bell described his feelings:

> Even some weeks after the event, I am unable to rationally express the range of my feelings—from abject humiliation to absolute outrage. Here were black students, some of whom had hailed my visit as a real gain for them, forced to bring me the news that even as I taught my courses, walked through the halls, attended meetings, and generally participated in the life of this community, a large percentage of students knew that the administration had

approved a program organized and specifically designed to compensate for student-reported teaching
inadequacies. It was by a considerable margin, the
worst moment of my professional life.[19]

Bell's experience is what I fear most about incorporating
Knefelkamp's advice into our formal peer review: that creative and progressive teaching will be suppressed. What
happened to Bell is very alarming to me. Because of his
nontraditional pedagogy and his frankness about race,
other faculty members assumed a lack of competence, and
literally resorted to teaching his Con Law course behind
his back. Let's face it: Derrick Bell is a famous man; even
though he is a black man, he has a lot of prestige and
power. If they would do this to Derrick Bell, Deborah, what
would they do to you and me?

So you are going to be willing to pass judgment on a
colleague's teaching goals, and I am not. We aren't going
to resolve our disagreement on this matter, which is fine
with me; our little word war is one of the pleasures of my
life. And since it is so much more fun disagreeing with
you, I will not extol the virtues of having learned all this
cognitive theory. That can be your winter's tale. All I
wanted to do in these hibernal reveries was to alert you to
the threat that the theories of Perry and Knefelkamp pose
to the privacy of the classroom. Many of our colleagues
would balk at being forced to explain and justify their
teaching theories and practices. I am not one of them. I
would welcome such a project, but confess that my feet
turn cold at the thought of dream assessment. I feel the

privacy of my own work as a teacher being invaded, and I do not like that. It is not the gnawing away at power that I dread, but the corrosion of creativity.

I have been thinking too, as I sit around the hearth on this long, dark night, of the parking lot faces. Do you remember that musing? I had it one morning last winter, when we were both working at the computers in the faculty research center. I was drinking tea and daydreaming, watching snow flurries and our colleagues in the faculty parking lot getting out of their cars—anything to avoid writing. You were, of course, in the middle of a maelstrom of ideas and words, and while you hummed "Uh huh" over your shoulder at the time, I didn't know if the musing registered, so I wrote it down:

> There is a very thin, diaphanous membrane be-
> tween a teacher's public and private life through
> which the body, the mind, and sometimes the soul,
> must pass, in and out, out and in, over and over
> again. For many of my colleagues, most of them
> male, the process does not seem to pose a problem.
> I am convinced that something happens to them in
> the parking lot, a metamorphosis, a mysterious and
> invisible process, that for some reason I lack the
> apparatus to perceive.
>
> From behind the Venetian blinds, I watch them
> at their cars, many of my colleagues, most of them
> male, dropping books on the asphalt, locking doors,
> pulling at wrinkled pants, smoothing rebellious
> hair. The faces that emerge from those cars seem

preoccupied, dubious about the morning they are in, dubious about the bodies they are in; there is an aura of dishevelment, bewilderment, and uncertainty.

But then they disappear, where my view of their journey is occluded by brick, and I cannot see them again unless I get up from my chair and go to greet them when they have entered the law school building. Lo and behold: they have new faces. Self-doubt has been replaced by an almost alarming confidence. They wear their authority with pleasure and ease, comfortable in the persona of law professor. Their books no longer tumble, and something has happened to their parking lot wrinkles, those wrinkles in their pants and on their worried faces. They are gone. Their faces are smooth, like rocks pounded by the surf—and hard. They wear smiles now, professional and condescending, with fiberglass lips designed for cool courtesy and the rule against perpetuities.

They must be getting those faces from somewhere, many of my colleagues, most of them male. Perhaps there is a hidden vending machine, dispensing new faces to law teachers as they round the corner and enter the building. Why can't I find this machine? Why is this product not available to me? Does it have something to do with gender? Would I want such a product, even if it were available? How can they teach with those other faces on?

Maybe there isn't just a vending machine in the

corner, but a more elaborate service as well, like a coat checking stand in a fancy restaurant. After all, where do their parking lot faces go when many of my colleagues, most of them male, cross the threshold of the law school? Maybe they peel their parking lot faces off, shedding their doubt and uncertainty, and hand them to a coat checker who puts a tag on them, and places them gingerly on a stainless steel rack. Is there some metaphysical bailee who takes possession of their vulnerability?

More than anything else, Deborah, that vending machine and the face checking stand caused our project on cognitive theory to fail with our colleagues. Learning how to become a better teacher requires a parking lot face. The parking lot face—a face that worries about one's place in the world—may not be an easy one to live behind. But that other law teacher face, the face they picked up from the vending machine, is nothing but mask. Can the wearer of that mask look out through those eyes—to navigate his way through the hallways, find his classroom and his place to teach?

I may never know, since wearing the mask is denied to me. But while I may never know whether the wearer of that mask can look out, I do know he cannot see within.

EIGHT

Winter

THE PROMISE OF SPRING: CRITICAL THINKING ABOUT COGNITIVE THEORY

When we were both renters, living across from the harbors in Halesite and Northport, respectively, you told me that winter was your favorite season. You looked forward to the time of year when the trees lost their leaves and the beauty of their bare limbs was finally evident. Leaves obscured your view of the harbor, of the water, and the wind at work. Winter meant an unobstructed view.

Now that we have entered metaphorical winter, the

point at which we reflect on what went before—the retreat, the research, and now the writing—I feel a similar sense of liberation and relief. Detail, even something as beautiful as the laciness of sycamore, or the complexity of cognitive theory, can make you feel claustrophobic. Here in winter, I hope we will have a clearer view.

In our research and now in our writing, we have chosen to explore our own intellectual development as well as that of our students. We are students exploring the domain of cognitive science, and there is a test—we have to write a book about our findings. Is this experiential learning, this process of empathizing with the subject (in our case, the student) and participating with the subject in the enterprise we are studying (education)?[1]

We have decided not to build walls between the observer and the observed, but to bring the personal and the professional into full view, exploring the relationship between the subjective and the objective, making public what is private—the meanings we assign to experiences, the way we interpret our world. Our whole project finds expression in a form of introspective writing.

The difference in our thinking is most obvious in the way we write, Louise. We knew collaboration would be difficult because we have different schedules, projects, and responsibilities. We work at a different pace even when we are both working, and we have different styles.

One of the differences in the way we work involves the way you use what you call "snidbits" of time, what I might call the "cracks" in the day, for your writing. I never imagined this practice could be explained as a cultural legacy of the Puritans. I just thought of it as one of the strategies we women use to juggle our responsibilities: family and career. Of course, it is highly unlikely that the sort of administrative skill you evidence in this juggling act will ever be classified as a higher form of intelligence. I think, though, that it qualifies as a form of Integration—an example of the way we bring different kinds of intelligence to bear in solving professional problems and life's problems.

Or perhaps, as you suggest, it is an example of Perry's Commitment. Perry holds John Bunyan's Pilgrim out as a role model for those who aspire to Commitment. If I had my way, that Pilgrim would have a different tale to tell. No longer would he be allowed to leave his family behind as he set out on his journey. He would have had to take his wife and children along, kicking and screaming all the way, on his long journey to redemption.

You mistake my sadness, Louise. What saddens me is not the ethic that deplores idle hands (although I concede that I view "idle" time as an essential part of the creative process) but your unwillingness to concede your own physical limits. When your snidbits of time are one to three in the morning and you have to get up at six to see your oldest off to school, I assume a physical cost is exacted.

I also know this choice is yours. Questioning your judgment in matters that are personal and private poses too much risk to our friendship. It is better to look sad than to say anything. I have learned over time that there are lines in friendship that should not be crossed, lines that mark the areas of possible misunderstanding, places where values collide in a way that can damage both sides. Maybe this issue of time management is one of those areas.

Perhaps I am wrong, Louise, but I am going to assume that there is no real conflict here. There is only misunderstanding. Your read my sadness as a criticism and I read your statement about the puritan ethic, despite your protestations to the contrary, as criticism, as an invocation of cultural hegemony. I know you do not mean to suggest that I am less industrious or that your way of working is somehow superior to the strategy I employ. But the assertion of superiority that you do not intend is embedded in the term "puritan ethic." The dominant culture assumes Puritans invented the work ethic or that they and their descendants have some sort of monopoly on this particular ethic.

I trace my ancestry to Guinea, West Africa, by way of Culpepper, Virginia, rather than England and the Massachusetts shore. I can't say with any certainty where John Waire or his ancestors set foot on this continent, but I know it wasn't Plymouth Rock. I do know that he and Elizabeth DuBois, his wife, his children and his children's children all know the meaning of hard work.

The hard work in my parents' and grandparents' generation involved physical labor. My father's school records describe his father's occupation as "laborer." When they weren't on strike in the 1950s, my father worked at Crucible Steel, where he was a steel "grinder." And it was my father who made sure I understood that there are different kinds of work, some more rewarding and desirable than others. When I tried coming home from school one day claiming illness, he put me to work mopping floors. To understand the magnitude of this punishment, you have to know that my father always maintained that mopping floors was heavy labor, something that should be done by men, not women.

Any expression of disapproval by my father was devastating. The bonds between us were strong—a man and his first-born child, his eldest daughter. Another one of the bonds between my father and me was intellectual. I was my father's friendly critic and his scrivener. I transcribed his poetry and mailed it off for publication in the church newspaper. I brought home my academic trophies (they actually gave out medals in those days for receiving the highest grade in a class or in a course) and displayed them for the pleasure of both my parents, but especially for my father. He had been a good student, the "brilliant" one in the family. He consistently earned As and Bs in conduct and reading, spelling and language. We had this in common.

The mystery for me as a child was why my father ended up with a job as a steelworker. I have a better sense of how this could be so, now that I have lived through two very public debates about the intellectual inferiority of Blacks, now that I can place his life in a particular historical context. My father entered school a year after *Birth of a Nation* recorded the ugly face of racism and presented it as history and patriotism. It is quite possible he sat through classes in which teachers discussed the scientific evidence, the analysis of the results of the Army's Alpha tests, which "proved" the inferiority of Negroes and foreign-born whites.[2] Given the immense popularity of the theories that proclaimed the intellectual inferiority of Blacks and Mexicans, among others, and the superiority of the Aryan or Nordic races, I was not surprised to learn recently that my father eventually said something that so offended a science teacher that the teacher hit him. Nor was I surprised to hear that my father hit the teacher back, packed up his books, and left school forever.

I was surprised when my sister relived this experience forty years later. She led a protest against the exclusion of Black students from the cheerleading squad and found herself tracked into a non-Regents program, a course of studies that would make it difficult for her to go to college. Her English teacher acted as her advocate and my sister pursued administrative relief. When she lost, the teacher handed her a copy of Richard Wright's book *Native Son* and advised her to leave the school.

That teacher saved my sister from my father's fate, I think. What he gave her was his faith in her worth as an intellectual and confirmation that what occurred in her case was not just, that it was racist and illegitimate. She says there are no words that can describe how emotionally devastated she was. But she survived. She had to leave our small town and travel to the next city to get a high school diploma, but she made it to college and graduated from law school.

I was in college when all this happened, a mere three hundred miles away, but for all I knew of those events I might as well have been in a different universe. I wish I had been there to fight for my sister. I wish my father had someone like my sister's teacher to fight for him. What happened to them both is often on my mind when I think about teaching. I would like to persuade students like my father and my sister to help me plant this garden of ours.

Sometimes I will have to persuade them that their seeds are not defective, that they don't have to worry about a garden full of weeds or puny stunted versions of the floral grandeur they see in the neighbors yards. Sometimes I will have to persuade them that they are not doomed to failure because they prefer to work in a different way from their industrious neighbors. I may have to remind them of our shared history. We know what it is to sow seeds and harvest a crop, and after all, this is just another field of endeavor.

Sometimes, Louise, you refer to the differences in the way we think categorically. You claim to be a linear thinker. I am not sure what that makes me. What kind of thinking is "not linear"? Do we have a name for it?

I am always troubled by this comparison. You remember when our reading group, the Weird Book Club, read Louise Erdrich's book *Tracks?*[3] A colleague said he couldn't finish the book. It was too hard to read. You agreed that the book was difficult although you at least persevered and finished the book. And then you explained that you thought linear thinkers would have a hard time with the book. Ordinarily I might have commented on the differences between you and him in your respective attitudes toward an "assignment," even one voluntarily undertaken for entertainment and mutual edification. But I must admit, I was too busy being stunned by your mutual confession of linearity to say anything at all.

I read *Tracks* in one sitting, completely engrossed in the mysteries of Pauline and Fleur Piliger. "Difficult" is the last word I would use to describe this book. And what made your assessment even more baffling was my recollection of our experience as a book group. We have waded through dense passages written by Borges, Camus, Joyce, and Kafka, and I don't remember anyone linking complaints about the difficulty of the reading to the nonlinear way the authors wrote or thought. If *Tracks* is hard for linear thinkers, as you say, does this mean that communication between linear thinkers and those who think like Louise Erdrich and maybe me (since I didn't have any trouble understanding her) will be difficult? Say it ain't so, Louise.

Gregory Bateson has a great line in his book *Steps to an Ecology of Mind.*[4] He tells the reader that his students were convinced he was hiding something from them, something that would make what he said to them intelligible. They were unable to understand what he had to teach them, Bateson concluded, because his way of thinking was different from theirs. But he wasn't talking about linear thinking versus something else. He was talking about the difference between inductive and deductive reasoning. "Reasoning," "rationality," and "linearity" are often used as though they are interchangeable. But, of course, they are not, and after reading all this material on cognitive theory, I am not sure we can reduce our differences to a simple dichotomy: linear thinker on one side, nonlinear thinker on the other.

Actually, nonlinear thinking has a name: holistic thinking. Having a name gives you a certain status, a certain legitimacy. Those who write about critical pedagogy claim that holism is the ability to see the "implicate order," the overall structure of a set of relationships, the ability to consider all things at once.[5] It sounds as though there might be some sort of reverse privileging going on here, or perhaps this description of holistic thinking is another example of the influence Eastern philosophy has on Western thinking. Enlightenment in the Eastern tradition has been described as the ability to "perceive the inexpressible nature of undifferentiated reality."[6]

Even though I am supposed to be the holistic thinker in our duo, I would never say that I am able to consider all things at once. You know me. I am strictly linear in the way I proceed to handle tasks. I like to finish one project before I begin another, and I find it impossible to write two things at the same time. But I do see connections that other people do not see and sometimes the connections are so thick and tightly woven, so overwhelming, that it is hard to know where to begin a discussion of a topic—like corporations or contracts or learning theory.

I would say that it is probably possible to be both linear and holistic, just as it is possible to be both abstract and concrete or reflective and active. But linearity was, and probably still is, the standard against which all thinking is measured. Linearity has invaded our popular consciousness in a way that makes it hard to understand what is meant by "linear" thinking. Linearity is a way of describing the way we perceive time and our place in the universe and much more.

I recently read an interview with Jodie Foster in which she said that her comedic role in *Maverick* was not as linear as her dramatic roles. Comedy is more freewheeling, while drama requires sustained concentration and planning. Maybe these are my taxonomizers, Louise. Discipline and improvisation as stand-ins for the conscious and unconscious or structure and chaos—these could be the paired characteristics that can be used to classify and describe different kinds of thought.

A linear thinker might want structure. Sitting at your dining room table, surrounded by toys and diapers and Dan's papers, I watch you struggle to impose order on this project. Your structure is the picture you have in your mind of the way the piece should work. You draw a diagram. Not an ordinary diagram, not lines or boxes, but an X. Before my eyes, the X is transformed into a butterfly. I listen as you vocalize the visual image you have, the way you divide up the ideas as if you were dividing up space, packing for a journey and deciding where to stow the luggage, placing a part of each task on each wing and even distributing some of the weight on the head of the poor fragile butterfly.

You think in metaphors, Louise. Metaphors are everywhere in your work and you use them slowly, deliberately, sounding out the words and playing with the analogies. You say you want to decorate the structure of our collaboration, to make it so beautiful and so enticing that people will enter and look around, unaware of the way the structure directs their attention, moves them along a pathway they don't see. I am reminded of something A. S. Byatt has written:

> It is not at all impossible, it is even common, not to think about the distance between words and things, between words and life, between words and reality. ... Language runs up and down, through and around things known and things imitated in a way paint doesn't . . . words are our common currency. We all have words.[7]

Is the well-written metaphor the goal of a linear thinker or a poet? Do linear thinkers think in metaphors? Do they think and write in ways that are both lyrical and melodious when heard in the mind, beautiful when they are seen with the mind's eye? Within the discipline of rhetoric, metaphor is said to be not only the currency of poets, but the way the writer produces truth; it is "the artistic analogue of scientific law."[8] Metaphor allows one to be both creative and authentic.[9]

There is a connection between metaphor and logic—one you seem to recognize despite your stated aversion to all things numerical. One of the books I read discussed the metaphors used by mathematicians that equate math with truth and beauty. Mathematics is a metaphor for order and rationality and beauty "unsullied by the passions."[10] I am amazed at this discussion of "reason's dream," this image of mathematics as a fantasy of order, "this dream of power, control, order, omnipotence."[11] Can you reject the metaphor and still lay claim to its power? Is there some form of logic that is not mathematical?

Even Gardner is no help here. He too has classified the multiple forms of intelligence and grouped three as "higher-level capacities": common sense, originality, and metaphoric capacity. His use of the term "metaphor" seems broad. It is defined as the capacity to draw analogies and to see connections, to "cut across different intellectual domains." And he speculates that "metaphoric ability" may be the "particular hallmark of logical mathematical intelligence to perceive patterns wherever they may be."[12]

I have always thought that math is linear. I was taught to do math in a linear way, the way you expect your students to proceed through a Property examination. There was a sequence to it. Gardner seems to think there is some connection between mathematics and metaphor, and maybe that means metaphor is linear. Maybe you are right, Louise. Maybe you are a linear thinker.

Linear thinkers, I have always assumed, are people who order the world in a sequential way, vertically, from introduction to conclusion, with one idea following logically from another. Is it the relationship between linearity and logic that fascinates me? Or rather, is it the absence of any sort of obvious relationship between logic and linearity in your visualization of this project that fascinates me? Linearity is associated with precision and rationality, but your butterfly is both precise and rational and not particularly linear.

For my part, I could care less about structure, at least at the beginning of a project. We both know that my tolerance for intellectual chaos is greater than yours. And I prefer to be surprised. I like reading what we have written and discovering the way we think alike and the places where we part company, where our paths diverge completely and how they wind around and meet again, crossing or con-joining, sometimes the same and sometimes separate but parallel. I prefer to find the structure our work suggests. And I prefer a different literary device, narrative. I like to tell stories. I think of stories as a form of logic, and that is why I use them.

I hoped when we began this project that cognitive the-ory would explain not only how we succeed or fail as teach-ers, but the significance of the differences in the way you and I think. If I balked at using Perry's theory, it was not because I did not understand Lee Knefelkamp's lecture. It was suspicion and political conviction that made me reflec-tive, not a predisposition in my cognitive style. Nor can I say that your choice to take what we had and work with it, to turn it into a piece of art, a work of scholarship, is evidence of your intellectual predisposition for the concrete rather than the abstract. It had more to do with the de-mands of a dissertation and three little girls than anything else. And you know what? I don't think we are alone in our improvisations.[13]

If there are certain irreducible differences, things that I can see and you cannot and vice versa, or different mean-ings we assign to events or physical phenomena or different feelings about the right or wrong of things, Perry certainly doesn't explain them. Do you remember how we spent hours talking about one line I had written in the description of the retreat? "There were no women among the men who were resolute in their intention to maintain their own credibility." You insisted the sentence was incomprehensi-ble; you could not understand what I was saying. And I was furious. My reaction was predictable because you sounded just like one of my students. What did I say that was so hard to understand? Like the contemporary cliché, "What part of no don't you understand?" I wanted to ask, "What is it you cannot understand about a simple description of the gendered reaction to your dilemma?" So we talked about it and talked about it, and you kept insisting that there cannot be any "women among men." It wasn't until you mentioned that men were a "class" that I finally understood your objection.

I imagine a room in which a line is drawn down the middle. On one side there are many women and some men. This is the side where the people who will admit they are wrong are seated. On the other side of the room, we find the people who will not admit they have made a mistake. Only men are seated on this side of the room. There are no women among these men.

In your mind, there is a class: "men who will not admit they are wrong." In this class, there can be no women. The class is defined in a way that precludes this possibility. Your way of understanding this particular sentence may be something that is peculiar to Property teachers; all those years of teaching future interests and the rule against perpetuities must affect your perception. Or perhaps you know some grammatical rule that I missed back in junior high when I was parsing sentences and learning how to conjugate verbs. Would you understand if I changed "among" to "amidst"? I don't know the basis, semantically, for our differences. I do know that if I were taking the multiple-choice part of your Property examination, I would be worried.

Nor could I understand your unwavering decision to use the Perry scheme. In fact, although there are parts of Perry's theory I find insightful and persuasive, the undifferentiated, unilinear, hierarchical structure of his scheme bothers me. I find it hard to imagine how our cognitive differences fit within this scheme. And if we belong in different categories, we won't be side by side. One of us will have a commanding view of the top of the other's head while the other will have a permanent crick in her neck from straining to look up.

The hierarchical nature of the scheme was evident from the first, but since the scheme is developmental, the application to students seemed appropriate. The first time I read Perry, there didn't seem to be anything in his description of the transitions from one stage to another to suggest that people of average intelligence are incapable of moving from Dualism to Multiplicity or to Contextual Relativism or Commitment. I thought the only impediment to this movement would be the resistance put up by the student, resistance rooted in what had been learned before.

That may not seem like such a radical proposition, but there are many of our colleagues who assert that some people "just are not smart enough" to be in law school, or sometimes, when they are more tactful, that there are some people who are not "adequately prepared" for law school.[14] And when I reread Perry carefully, I discovered that he does not disagree with these propositions. While

Perry's theory doesn't feel like a judgment that can be translated into rules of inclusion and exclusion, it can be used that way. Intellect is a measure of entitlement. Those who deserve an education get it. Those who deserve a Harvard education get it. Those who have merit succeed.

Perhaps I would find these comments less objectionable if I believed that discussions of difference and competence were less dependent on a personal preference for criteria that measure ability in a way that is self-validating. We have convinced ourselves that our methods of selection are capable of sorting the most qualified from the least qualified, and in the process, the standard that measures success on law school exams becomes a measure of native intelligence, a credential asked for in the employment interview.[15]

It matters where you are in Perry's scheme. It matters when Perry concludes that some people have "emotional controls so bound up with an internalization of the all or nothing, authority oriented structures . . . that they cannot contemplate change without overwhelming anxiety" and that others have "a particular style of cognition, information processing or learning" that "may be relatively resistant to change and of a kind that do not support the skills required by the strategies we invite them to learn."[16] Who are these people who have "styles" that will not "support a skill" that is needed to learn a "strategy"? If Perry had known me as an undergraduate, would he have written me off?

Lee Knefelkamp did have an answer to my question "How do we get our students from stage 1 to stage 4?"

She is too good a teacher to be without one. It is a simple four-part description of our task, a list of things to do: create a classroom with structure, experiential learning, diversity, and personalism.[17] Lee Knefelkamp reassures us that Perry's scheme is not threatening because the strength in Perry's model is the presence of the students' voices. In Perry's work there is respect for the student, for his or her courage in tackling the "ego-threatening" task of educating him- or herself.

Intellectual and moral development are connected in Perry's scheme, both in the student's development and in the teacher's responsibility. You can't disavow all moral judgments, Louise, and embrace Perry (or rather Knefelkamp). Part of the appeal of their work is the way they seem to care about students. This is a "student-centered" theory, one created by a person who listened carefully to what students had to say about their experience in college. Perry's theory asks us to try and understand what a student feels, to understand the sense of loss experienced when he or she confronts uncertainty or contradiction. We are exhorted to listen and to hear the students' expressions of loss; to help them make transitions by acting as "a bridge linking the old self with the new"; and finally to teach by example, to show them order and disorder (unresolved dilemmas) in our own disciplines, to "validate for our students a dialectical mode of thought which at first seems irrational and then to assist them in honoring its limits."[18]

I wonder if Perry or Knefelkamp read law reviews, whether they have read the articles in which James Elkins describes his first-year students' journals.[19] Their journals show first-year law students deeply mired in the first or second stage of Perry's theory. They are full of fear: fear of arbitrariness, the fear of failure, the fear that ensures failure. They are angry and frustrated. They know that success means a splintering of self, a division into the professional and the personal to mirror the dichotomies that dominate the first-year curriculum—theoretical and practical, procedural and substantive, public and private law.

My Civil Procedure professor in my first year of law school was Jan Vetter, a visitor at Harvard from Berkeley's Boalt Hall. In a ritual of intimacy that Harvard must have designed, several other students and I were invited to lunch by Jan Vetter. I suppose it was his job to make sure that Harvard was not perceived as an impersonal place with uncaring faculty. At lunch he told us about a change that would take place, how we were already becoming very different people. This revelation was met with nods and shared stories about how much more adversarial and argumentative we were already becoming with family and friends.

I have always wanted to tell Jan Vetter that he was wrong. If there was a change, it was only temporary. Oh, I have a different persona now, something like that parking lot face, which I put on when I am in an adversarial situation. I sometimes put on this persona in the classroom, like armor, but not often. It is something I wear, not part of who I am.

I found out the hard way, I might add, that my values really were not altered by law school. I may have embarked on my career as a corporate lawyer, but I really did not have the heart for it. I did not see the humor in calling the investing public "mullets," silly fish that practically jump into your boat when you are fishing in the Gulf of Mexico. What humor is there in suggesting that compliance with federal securities laws allows you to bilk widows and orphans out of their savings? The jokes were far too close to the truth for my liking. My perception of right and wrong, my conception of justice, had not really changed all that much.

We force students into relativism by challenging their belief systems and values. The adversarial model demands the exposition of counterarguments.[20] If the students resist, they are prodded along by what we call the Socratic method. Law school is something to be feared because other people have the power to hurt you. Elkins's students, my students, your students, Louise—they all cling to the idea that their survival is a matter of pleasing someone else.

Law students cannot derive meaning from this process, unless the meaning is the one supplied by Early Multiplicity, the belief that every opinion is valid, every decision a matter of personal morality, and the only thing that matters is power. All law teachers have stories about that moment teaching their first-year class when the students realize there is no "rule" to decide the outcome in a particular case. Some students view this as a kind of betrayal, while others greet this knowledge with cynicism, confirmation of their suspicion that judges are completely arbitrary and extraordinarily powerful.

The students describe law school as a transformative experience. They are very clear about the first stage, the stage that separates them from the person they were in the past, loosening the grip of a sense of right and wrong, abandoning what they knew before. They recognize law school as a rite of passage. Peter McLaren suggests that we make this explicit and that we examine the role ritual should play in education. He would probably characterize the first year of law school as liminal, a "great moment of teachability."

A rite of passage moves the initiates across a social distance.[21] The in-between stage is liminality, the point of reentry is reaggregation or reintegration. Perry talks about our role as teachers, as a bridge between our students' old and new selves. The parallel between the description of Perry's scheme and the description of the cultural phenomenon known as a rite of passage is neither casual nor coincidental. But I am afraid we have abandoned our students, left them afloat in a liminal sea too far out to return to Dualism, to the certainty and security of that shore, and too far from Commitment to think about swimming to the other side.

I had a student last year in Sociology of Law who took the class discussion of ritual and incorporated it into her paper on parenting and the legal rules with respect to the termination of parental rights. She made the argument that a good parent was one who knew how to create and conduct rituals. Perhaps she was inspired by our team teaching, Louise, or by your writing on ritual,[22] or by a classmate's description of the daily ritual he performs before going to bed, checking all windows and doors, locking up the house and looking in on each of his children—a ritual that signifies a desire to protect them through the night, to keep them safe. The ritual is important to him, an expression of what he perceived as his duty. The meaning his children assigned to this ritual was equally important.

Parents are supposed to guide their children from infancy to adulthood. I don't think teaching is analogous to parenting, and I reject the metaphor of teacher as midwife that has been offered up by feminist scholars in the field of cognitive theory and the law.[23] I object to this metaphor not because it is gendered, a criticism that has been answered, but because I just don't see our job as one where we assist at a birth. A midwife's job is done when the baby is born, when the child emerges from the mother and becomes something separate and distinct. This is too much like the splintering of self first-year students fear. It is too much like the arguments made by those who distinguish personal and professional morality.

Learning shouldn't separate us from ourselves, although it may transform us in the sense that it brings us closer to understanding who we are and what we are capable of achieving in our lives. I am willing to accept the designation of guide, to affirm what is figuratively or literally an intergenerational enterprise. McLaren thinks we should think of ourselves as liminal servants ever cognizant of our shamanic roots. What excites me most about this description of teaching is the suggestion that if we embrace this approach, we also embrace the idea of metaphoric teaching, that this "could lead to knowledge that is danced."[24]

The description of our role in this process of reintegration and identification is daunting. I am not sure that I am up to being "charismatic," but I am willing to work at intimacy, even in a class of over a hundred students.[25] I want to bring them safely through to Commitment.

Getting to Commitment is painful, for the student and for me. It is not the threat to our egos that is painful, it is learning how to think. Many of our colleagues would argue that we are not responsible for the pain we see among our students. Perry described the place between stages as transitions, and transitions are always painful.

But you see, we create uncertainty for the student; we cast doubt on ideas assumed to be true for an entire lifetime, however short or long that might be. What we do in the classroom, Louise, is to challenge our students' worldviews. The challenge is implicit in something as simple as pointing out the flaws in the way a decision is written, or in your decision to assign problems that involve dinosaur bones and African American cemeteries and issues of equitable distribution in a divorce, or in your very presence in the classroom.

And we both know how hard it is to deal with the pain of our students when that pain has made them vicious, when they lash out with a visceral reaction to something we say or don't say, something we do or don't do—launching attacks that are nothing more than name-calling: witch, socialist, militant feminist, femi-nazi. But Perry has demanded that we do as much as we can to alleviate the pain. It would be more than irresponsible to ignore the pain; it would be immoral.

There is no possibility for learning when a mind shuts down. A student may hold his values up to the light, shake them out, examine them for defects or flaws, and having found none, decide that they are perfectly good and will serve for a lifetime. This could be the student who decides that whatever the cost to particular individuals, we are all better served by limited government. I have had students like that in my classes, students who were prepared and willing to debate the meaning of the First Amendment or the benefits of formalism in contract law. But for every student who is prepared to accept the responsibilities of Commitment, to cooperate with us in our attempt to plant a garden, we have more than one who resembles your "shell-less mottled mollusks, shrinking from the sun.

I am not sure how we lure a cringing student out into the sunlight. I do know that we don't have much chance of succeeding if we engage in the kind of rituals that inflict pain gratuitously. Peter McLaren has written about these rituals of pain. His description of a Catholic secondary school serves equally well as a description of some of the techniques employed in law school:

> Tacit methods of inflicting pain can come from . . . insults or caustic comments from teachers, ignoring students' raised hands, or somber and blank facial features when speaking to a student. By far the most common tactic employed by teachers . . . was that of embarrassing the students. Concerted attempts at deflating them, chipping away at their sense of security or identity.[26]

Although most of the pain he described was psychological, one form of punishment was both psychological and

199

physical, "the pain of censure if one requested to attend to one's bodily functions at an inappropriate time." [27]

A couple of years ago, a pregnant student, a Black woman, came to me in tears because she had just been marked absent in one of her courses. The teacher had a rule that if you were not in your seat when he called roll, you were marked absent. Frequent trips to the restroom are imperative during pregnancy, and so this student asked for permission to leave. He said she was free to leave, but he would have to mark her absent. Now, as far as I can tell, this faculty member has never admitted he was wrong or that there might be some problem in having a rule that penalizes a student who wishes to use the bathroom. He was willing to handle this particular student's problems privately, as long as none of the other students found out about his modification of his rules. I think he probably views pain as an integral part of a rite of passage.

I know you disagree with him. You've said as much more than once, and your difference of opinion is a matter of public record. You may not know the circumstances of the woman who slapped the child in the grocery store (although I think more likely that it is knowledge of women who shop with children that makes you so charitable), but you certainly know and understand the circumstances of those who walk into a law school classroom. You do not engage in rituals of pain to confirm your own power and you criticize those who do.

I think we teach our students about Commitment, Louise. Admittedly, it is hard to teach.[28] Whether we call it Commitment, Integration, or wisdom, at some point our students should learn to make judgments. They ought to be offered opportunities to watch others make judgments and to make their own. Perhaps we could begin by acknowledging our own commitment, creating what Knefelkamp calls a "generative" community, a community that takes responsibility for what it creates.[29] Perhaps we could go beyond that and consider whether we want to be "transformative intellectuals," whether we will admit that our institutions are "economic, cultural and social sites that are inextricably tied to the issues of control and power."[30]

Like it or not, we make judgments all the time, and if our judgments are not arbitrary, then we are acting on a belief—our commitment to a set of ideals. We decide how we will vote on appointments, retention, tenure, and promotion matters. We evaluate our colleagues' teaching and writing. It is just that up until now, our commitment often has been expressed as a form of opposition—to sexism or racism or the manipulation of existing standards. We fulfill the role Chinua Achebe has assigned to poets and writers, paradigmatic outsiders, advocating some sort of social transformation.[31] And what happens if that transformation occurs? Do we lose our standing as writers, as artists, as poets?

I don't think we have to worry about that for a while, at least. We can't avoid the nastiness of politics because schools are the places where ideas are most likely to be contested. And as things stand, we are right in the middle of that contest. No matter how much someone like Richard Epstein tries to manipulate the categories, to engage in a process of inversion in imagery and logic, white men are neither outsiders nor are they at risk of exclusion.[32] On the other hand, the movement to end affirmative action is like one of those high-speed trains. We both know what that means. Principles of academic freedom are no protection when people with power decide that they do not want to share, that they don't want to be fair.

When that happens, I think it is our duty to confront them with the Truth. Truth is not personal and private; it is shared and public even though it is contextual. Yes, I believe in Truth with a capital T. Most of the time, the criticism directed at my work by the people whose words and actions I describe in my writing has to do with the way I have interpreted their words or conduct. My interpretation is guided by my belief that the truth is found in a perspective that sees both what the dominant discourse would have us see and what those who are outside and underneath see as well. The "truth" is a vision recorded with a wide-angle lens. And when I feel compelled to describe this broader vision as truth, I usually find you there beside me, Louise.

We do make judgments, perhaps not about the way someone teaches, but certainly about his concern for students and his interest in teaching. Admit it, Louise, you are as deeply offended as I am when a colleague makes no effort to conceal his lack of interest in his chosen profession, in the work that he does or the students who rely on him.

The point of the retreat was to learn how to be better teachers. If we have learned anything at all, it has to be that power and politics are not separate or different from teaching. They are at the heart of it. We have two choices.

We can reduce what we do to a routine, to something instrumental or technical, or we can affirm our role as intellectuals. We have the right to make judgments about the way others teach. We have a right to think critically. It is the kind of judgment Perry would expect of us if we want to graduate to Late Multiplicity.

This does not mean that I think there is one right way to teach. Nothing could be further from my mind. For example, I think we could use instruction in "technical" skills to reach students, to persuade them to make that move to level 4 or level 9 in Perry's scheme. It would capture their attention and move them beyond Dualism and "empty receptacle" reasoning while teaching them what they need to know about their chosen profession, how to solve problems for their clients.

We could do that, but I don't think that's the only way to improve our teaching. If anything, I think this exploration of cognitive theory and your experiment may have exposed the fallacy of our greatest obsession, the dichotomy between theory and "rules" of law. We have defined "skills" far too narrowly. Our arguments about the lines drawn between the practical and the theoretical and between the intellectual and the moral or ethical are distracting. They blind us to the choices we have made to emphasize one kind of intelligence or one cognitive style to the exclusion of all others, when the practice of law allows, in fact probably requires, competency in a much wider variety of both.

There is a refrain that runs through the reflection pieces of James Elkins's first-year students that troubles me greatly.[33] The lawyer is no poet. This plaint is reflected in the adjectives chosen to describe legal writing: technical, precise, efficient, emotionless, and uncreative.[34] The law student's only glimpse of escape from the tediousness of it all is appellate advocacy, where passion is permissible, where words may be used to persuade.

Why do they assume that law and poetry exist in opposition?[35] There is no more reason to believe that than there is to believe that reason and emotion exist only in opposition or that precision and creativity cannot coexist. We know it is possible to be both rational and passionate. Passion may be another word for commitment, the kind of commitment you have to your family, to your writing, to friendship, or to your students.

Different conceptions of order can be divisive. Apparently Albert Einstein and Neils Bohr ended their dialogue about physics because their theories of order were incompatible. The distance between the two men became the distance between quantum theory and relativity.[36] Do you think our conceptions of order are so different, Louise, that our friendship might be at risk?

We both love words. You prefer metaphors; I use stories. We each "know" the world in very different ways and yet we both are actively engaged in what Archibald MacLeish called the journey of the mind: looking for, thinking about, testing, comparing, caressing, and cherishing new ideas, trying to fit them into the larger picture of our lives.

MacLeish, poet and lawyer, distinguished between the ways the two professions use words. Lawyers may use words as symbols, but poets, he wrote, understand "the way words work as signs, objects, metaphors and images." [37] Perhaps this is the nature of our commitment, that in this world dominated by the visual, by color and sound, we still believe that if we teach our students to be good lawyers, they will move epistemologically and cognitively into the domain of the poet, a domain they believe they have abandoned.

"Insatiable fires in the mind" are what MacLeish found in law school. [38] The "socratic spark" lit the fire. [39] Maybe this is something we can't teach. Maybe it just happens on its own. Or perhaps, like those who built fires with tinder and stone, you just keep making sparks and hope the kindling will catch fire. You never know how long the ember will smolder before it bursts into flame.

LOUISE'S EPILOGUE

From the breakfast table I watch the dawn's light, pale and watery, pour onto the empty lawn. The tree branches still break black against the sky, but they are sleek and supple. It is late winter, almost early spring.

I am drinking tea, and once again browsing through my gardening book and seed catalogs, those harbingers of spring. The table is strewn with shiny pages splashed with yellows and purples and reds and blues—last year's successful flower beds in somebody else's garden. My book tells me what I am supposed to be doing at this time of year: planning my garden, determining the right number of plants, the amount of space the mature plants will need, and the times at which the particular varieties should be planted. There are charts of frost dates, warnings about gardens on north-facing hills, and exhortations to call the orchardist about the temperature and duration of that winter chill for the fruit trees I do not own. I marvel at my excitement: spring is going to come again, and I am still here, and maybe this year I will grow the perfect garden.

There is a chapter on insect pests, and I think about our project on cognitive theory last year. I am struck by the elegance of the lace bug, her filigree wings studded with minute cabochon aquamarines. She is a delicate thing, a "true bug," who has sucked the juice from the hirsute leaves of the marigold, leaving a golden patch behind her. She is also a pest. There are pages devoted to her extermination, and I am reminded of those beetles from the last solar cycle, of their shiny black backs and shimmering iridescence.

There is a chapter on weeds, defined as plants that are "growing in the wrong place." The status of weed is culturally determined. Tomatoes were once considered weeds, and thought to be poisonous; now we lavish them on hamburgers. In some gourmet gardens dandelions are raised as a valuable green, while in the garden next door they are soaked with herbicide. I have always loved dandelions, their burst of yellow sunshine, their sturdy purple stems, and the graceful way they age, silver spheres of fluff blown into the wind by the huffing and puffing of children.

On the first warm day, Deborah, would you like to go into the backyard and sit in the grass with me? The girls could play, and we could watch the spring roll in. Besides, I want to discuss with you this matter of pests and weeds— and maybe what we ought to do this year. You've got to see my new book on bulbs and dividing rhizomes. I can just imagine it now, from my breakfast table: a vast periwinkle sea of bearded irises.

Forget about waiting for the first warm day. Come over this morning, Deborah, and I'll make us a fresh pot of tea.

DEBORAH'S EPILOGUE

Louise, I can think of nothing lovelier than sharing a pot of tea with you on this early spring day. Our conversation is bound to stray from bearded irises, and other spring flowers, and I am sure we'll disagree about weeds and pests. One of us is going to argue for wildflower status for one weed or another. After all, how will we know when summer is here without Queen Anne's lace and chicory? And as for pests, what will the girls do while we're digging in the dirt if there are no pill bugs to play with?

Whatever we do today, over our cup of tea, landscaping your yard or mine—talking about wildflowers or cognition or children or law students—we are cultivating our own intelligence, planting seeds that will yield a harvest in the future. Nothing is really a digression when you include friendship, collaboration, and struggle among the flowers that you plant.

NOTES

NOTES TO CHAPTER TWO

1. The test turned out to be Charles Meisgeier and Elizabeth Murphy, *Type Indicator for Children* (Palo Alto: Consulting Psychologist Press, 1987).
2. My personal experiences are recounted in Deborah Waire Post, "Reflections on Identity, Diversity and Morality," *Berkeley Women's L. J.* 6 (1990–91): 136, a volume that also contains articles on the same or similar subjects by other members of the Northeast Corridor Collective of Black Women Law Professors.
3. Patricia Williams, *Alchemy of Race and Rights, Diary of a Law Professor* (Cambridge: Harvard University Press, 1991).
4. Regina Austin, "Sapphire Bound!" *Wis. L. Rev.* (1989): 539, 540.
5. Archibald MacLeish, "Apologia," *Harv. L. Rev.* 85 (1972): 1505.
6. See e.g., Roger C. Cramton, *Report and Recommendations of the Task Force on Lawyer Competency: The Role of the Law Schools, American Bar Association Section on Legal Education and Admission to the Bar* (Chicago: ABA Press, 1979).
7. Task Force on Law Schools and the Profession: Narrowing the Gap, Robert MacCrate (Chairman), *Legal Education and Professional Development: An Educational Continuum* (Chicago: Ameri-

can Bar Association, Section on Legal Education and Admissions to the Bar, 1992) (hereinafter cited as MacCrate Report).

8. MacCrate Report, 29–120.
9. Ann Scales, "Surviving Legal De-Education: An Outsider's Guide," *Vt. L. Rev.* 15 (1990): 139.
10. Fox Butterfield, "Harvard Law School Torn by Race Issue," *New York Times*, April 21, 1990. A law student criticized Regina Austin because he claimed she "showed favoritism toward minority students and women" and she had "an unconventional approach to teaching . . . teaching more sociology than law."
11. The MacCrate Report describes the "large firm phenomenon," the growth of the six hundred largest law firms, which "are the most prominent sector of the profession today," firms that "trace their origins to Wall Street not Main Street." MacCrate Report, 75.
12. Ibid., 81
13. Jeanne Glader, "Harvest of Shame: The Imposition of Independent Contractor Status on Migrant Farm Workers and Its Ramifications for Migrant Children," *Hastings L. J.* 42 (1991): 1455. Edward R. Morrow's exposé on farm workers is called "Harvest of Shame." A more recent documentary borrows the name and updates the stories of farm workers. *Frontline,* "New Harvest; Old Shame" (PBS Videos, 1990).
14. Printed with the permission of a student who wishes to remain anonymous. Reflection piece on file with the authors.
15. Louise Harmon, "Law, Art, and the Killing Jar," *Iowa L. Rev.* 79 (1994): 367.

NOTES TO CHAPTER THREE

1. Arthur E. Levine has recently become the ninth president of Teachers College, Columbia University, having resigned as the chairman of the Institute for Educational Management at Harvard's Graduate School of Education.
2. L. Lee Knefelkamp is a professor of higher education and the chair of the Higher and Adult Education Department at Teachers College, Columbia University.

3. My discussion is based on an article by William G. Perry, "Cognitive and Ethical Growth: The Making of Meaning," in *The Modern American College,* ed. Arthur Chickering and Associates (San Francisco: Jossey-Bass, 1981).

4. Ibid., 78.

5. Ibid.

6. Ibid., 80.

7. Ibid., 83.

8. Ibid.

9. Robert E. Lerner, *One Thousand Years: Western Europe in the Middle Ages* (Boston: Houghton Mifflin, 1974), 170.

10. Ibid., 171.

11. Perry, "Cognitive and Ethical Growth," 81.

12. From Hazel Weiser's teaching journal (currently on file with the authors).

13. Ibid.

14. Perry, "Cognitive and Ethical Growth," 83.

15. Ibid., 85.

16. Ibid., 83.

17. Ibid., 95.

18. Ibid.

19. Ibid.

20. Roger Cramton, "The Ordinary Religion of the Law School Classroom," *J. Legal Educ.* 29 (1977–78): 256.

21. Ibid., 256.

22. Peter McLaren, *Schooling as Ritual Performance* (Boston: Routledge & Kegan, 1986), 121–22.

NOTES TO CHAPTER FOUR

1. Professor Welty is professor of management at Pace University's Lubin Graduate School of Business, director of the Center for Faculty Development and Teaching Effectiveness, and codirector of the Center for Case Studies in Education. His research in teacher education has been funded by the Fund for the Improvement of Postsecondary Education (FIPSE), and the cases he developed have been published in a series. William Welty, Rita

Silverman, and Sally Lyon, *Case Studies for Teacher Problem Solving* (White Plains: Center for Case Studies, 1992).

2. Paolo Friere, *Pedagogy of the Oppressed* (New York: Seaburg Press, 1973), 180–86; Anthony Giddens, *Profiles and Critiques in Social Theory* (Los Angeles: University of California Press, 1982).

3. 1 Cor. 13:12 King James Version.

4. Louise Harmon, "Fragments on the Deathwatch," *Minn. L. Rev.* 77 (1992): 1.

5. Zora Neale Hurston, *The Sanctified Church: The Folklore Writing of Zora Neale Hurston* (Berkeley: Turtle Island Foundation, 1981).

6. Perry, "Cognitive and Ethical Growth," 79.

7. Ibid., 82.

8. Ibid., 96.

NOTES TO CHAPTER FIVE

1. Cynthia Davidson, "Legal Maneuvers," *Interiors,* June 1991, 74.

2. *A History of the School of Law, Columbia University* (New York: Columbia University Press, 1955), 138.

3. Ibid., 139.

4. C. A. Peairs, Jr., "Essay on the Teaching of Law," *J. Legal Educ.* 12 (1960): 369.

5. *The Centennial History of the Harvard Law School, 1817–1917* (Cambridge: The Harvard Law School Association, 1918), 76–77.

6. Christopher Columbus Langdell, *A Summary of the Law of Contracts* (Littleton, Colo.: Fred B. Rothman, 1980), iii.

7. *Centennial History of the Harvard Law School,* 76–77.

8. Calvin Woodward, "The Limits of Legal Realism: An Historical Perspective," *Va. L. Rev.* 54 (1968): 715–16.

9. Jerold S. Auerbach, "What Has the Teaching of Law to Do with Justice?" *N.Y.U. L. Rev.* 53 (1978): 458.

10. Ibid., 459.

11. *Centennial History of the Harvard Law School,* 36.

12. William M. O'Barr and John M. Conley, "Litigant Satisfaction versus Legal Adequacy in Small Claims Court Narratives," *Law & Society Rev.* 19 (Fall 1985): 661–701; and idem, "Rules versus

Relationships in Small Claims Disputes," in *Conflict Talk,* ed. A. Grimshaw (New York: Cambridge University Press, 1990).

13. Nadya Aisenberg and Mona Harrington, *Women of Academe: Outsiders in the Sacred Grove* (Amherst: University of Massachusetts Press, 1988), 76.

14. Thomas D. Eisele, "Wittgenstein's Instructive Narratives: Leaving the Lessons Latent," *J. Legal Educ.* 40 (1990): 89.

15. Christopher Chippendale, "The Snettisham Treasure: A Case of Uncommon Law," *Archeology,* March/April 1993.

16. Spencer P. M. Harrington, "Bones and Bureaucrats: New York's Great Cemetery Imbroglio," *Archeology,* March/April 1993.

17. *Black Hills Institute of Geological Research and Black Hills Museum of Natural History Foundations, Inc. v. the United States of America, Dept. of Justice,* 96 F. 2d 1237 (8th Cir. 1992).

18. *In re Marriage of Graham,* 574 P. 2d 75 (1978).

19. Jack Himmelstein, from "Reassessing Law Schooling: The Sterling Forest Group," *N.Y.U. L. Rev.* 53 (1978): 576.

20. See Jay M. Feinman, "Teaching Assistants," *J. Legal Educ.* 41 (1991): 274.

21. Elyce H. Zenoff and Jerome A. Barron, "So You Want to Hire a Law Professor?" *J. Legal Educ.* 33 (1983): 508.

NOTES TO CHAPTER SIX

1. L. Lee Knefelkamp, *Community of Scholars: College and Student Personnel Administration* (1980), 373.

2. Ibid., 23.

3. Howard Gardner, *Frames of Mind: The Theory of Multiple Intelligences* (New York: Basic Books, 1983).

4. Clyde Spillenger, "Reproduction and Medical Interventionism: An Historical Comment," *Nova L. Rev.* 13 (1989): 385; Dorothy E. Roberts, "Crime, Race and Reproduction," *Tul. L. Rev.* 67 (1993): 1945.

5. Richard Herrnstein and Charles Murray, *The Bell Curve* (New York: Free Press 1994). For documents and essays on the history of the IQ debate in the United States as well as essays critical of the Bell Curve, see Russell Jacoby and Naomi Glauberman, *The*

Bell Curve Debate: History, Documents, Opinions (New York: Times Books, 1995).

6. Clyde Kluckhohn, *Mirror for Man: A Survey of Human Behavior and Social Attitudes* (Greenwich, Conn.: Fawcett, 1964).

7. Margaret W. Matlin, *Cognition*, 3d ed. (Fort Worth, Tex.: Harcourt Brace Publishers, 1994).

8. Perry, "Cognitive and Ethical Growth," 96.

9. James Joyce, *A Portrait of the Artist as a Young Man* (New York: Viking, 1964).

10. Jay Feinman, "The Jurisprudence of Classification," *Stan. L. Rev.* 41 (1989): 710.

11. Robert M. Pirsig, *Zen and the Art of Motorcyle Maintenance* (New York: Bantam Books New Age, 1981), 252.

12. Ibid.

13. See, e.g., Gregory Williams, *Life on the Color Line* (New York: Dutton, 1995); Judy Scales Trent, *Notes of a White Black Woman: Race, Color, Community* (University Park: Pennsylvania State University Press, 1995).

14. Langston Hughes, "Who's Passing for Who?" in *Literature IV: The Oregon Curriculum/A Sequential Program in English* (New York: Holt, Rinehart and Winston, 1969).

15. Howard Gardner, *The Mind's New Science, A History of the Cognitive Revolution* (New York: Basic Books, Division of Harper Collins, 1987), 39.

16. Robbie Case, *Intellectual Development: Birth to Adulthood* (Orlando: Academic Press, 1985).

17. L. Lee Knefelkamp, "Faculty and Student Development in the 80's: Renewing the Community of Scholars," in *Integrating Adult Development Theory with Higher Education Practice,* 1980 Current Issues in Higher Education, no. 5 (Washington, D.C.: American Association for Higher Education, 1980).

18. David Klahr and J. G. Wallace, *Cognitive Development: An Information Processing View* (Hillsdale: Lawrence Erlbaum Associates, 1976).

19. See, e.g., Robert Ennis, "A Taxonomy of Critical Thinking Dispositions and Abilities," in *Teaching Thinking Skills: Theory and Practice* (New York: W. H. Freeman, 1987).

20. See, e.g., G. M. Seddon, "The Properties of Bloom's Taxonomy of Educational Objectives for the Cognitive Domain," *Review of Educational Research* 48 (spring 1978); see also the taxonomy of taxonomies described by Patrick C. Kyllonen and Valerie J. Shute, "A Taxonomy of Learning Skills," in *Learning and Individual Differences,* ed. Phillip Ackerman, Robert Sternberg, and Robert Glaser (New York: W. H. Freeman, 1989).

21. Janet Cornfield and L. Lee Knefelkamp, *Analysis of the Learner Characteristics of Students Implied by the Perry Scheme* (1979).

22. See Ennis, "Taxonomy."

23. David A. Kolb, "Learning Styles and Disciplinary Differences," in *The Modern American College,* ed. A. Chickering and Associates (San Francisco: Jossey-Bass, 1981).

24. Ibid., 233.

25. Ibid., 234.

26. For a summary of this debate, see John O. Mudd, "Beyond Rationalism: Performance Referenced Legal Education," *J. Legal Educ.* 35 (1986): 189.

27. Harry T. Edwards, "The Growing Disjunction between Legal Education and the Legal Profession," *Mich. L. Rev.* 91 (1992): 34.

28. Karl N. Llewellyn, *The Bramble Bush* (New York: Oceana Publications, 1951).

29. See also the discussion of human reasoning in Gardner, *Mind's New Science,* 360–80.

30. *Webb v. McGowin,* 27 Ala. App. 82, 168 So. 196 (1935); *Harrington v. Taylor,* 255 N.C. 690; 36 S.E. 2d 227 (1945).

31. Gardner, *Mind's New Science,* 367.

32. Ibid.

33. Richard D. Kahlenberg, *Broken Contract: A Memoir of Harvard Law School* (New York: Hill and Wang, Division of Farrar, Straus and Giroux, 1992).

34. Allan Collins, Eleanor H. Warnock, Nelleke Aiello, and Mark L. Miller, "Reasoning from Incomplete Knowledge," in *Representation and Understanding: Studies in Cognitive Science,* ed. Daniel G. Bobrow and Allan Collins (New York: Academic Press, 1975).

35. Ibid., 406.

36. Ibid.

37. Jim Krueger, "We Just Disagree," performed by Dave Mason, Columbia 3-10575.
38. *Prime Time,* "The Fairer Sex" (1990).
39. Kolb, "Learning Styles," 237–38.
40. Larry Richard, "How Personality Affects Your Practice: The Lawyer Types," *ABA Journal* (1993): 74–78.
41. Albert A. Canfield, *Learning Styles Inventory* (Los Angeles: Western Psychological Services, 1992).
42. Ibid., 24.
43. Ibid., 25.
44. Kolb, "Learning Styles," 250.
45. Paul B. Baltes, "The Aging Mind: Potential and Limits," *Gerontologist* 33 (1993): 580.
46. Pat Hutchings and Allen Wutzdorff, "Experiential Learning across the Curriculum: Assumptions and Principles," *New Directions for Teaching and Learning (Knowing and Doing; Learning through Experience)* 35 (1988): 5–19.
47. Perry, "Cognitive and Ethical Growth," 97.
48. Ibid.
49. Ibid.
50. Ibid., 96.
51. Ibid., quoting M. Basseches (unpublished dissertation), 96.
52. Kolb, "Learning Styles," 237.
53. Gardner, *Frames of Mind.*
54. Ibid., 170–204.
55. G. H. Colt, "The Polyhedral Arthur Loeb," *Harv. Mag.* 31 (March–April 1982), quoted in Gardner, *Frames of Mind,* 192.
56. Robert Sternberg and Richard K. Wagner, "Individual Differences in Practical Knowledge and Its Acquisition," in Ackerman, Sternberg, and Glaser, *Learning and Individual Differences.*

NOTES TO CHAPTER SEVEN

1. F. Kottenkamp, *The History of Chivalry and Armor,* trans. A. Löwy (New York: Portland House, 1988), 47.
2. *Lynch v. Indiana State University Board of Trustees,* 378 N.E. 2d 900 (1978).

3. Ibid., 903.
4. Ibid., 908.
5. *Martin v. Parrish,* 805 F. 2d 583 (5th Cir. 1986).
6. Ibid.
7. Ibid.
8. Ibid.
9. Ruth P. Knight, "Remembering," *J. Legal Educ.* 40 (1990): 102.
10. *Carley v. Arizona Bd. of Regents,* 737 P. 2d 1099 (1987).
11. Ibid., 1101.
12. Emil Oberholzer, "The Church in New England Society," in *Seventeenth-Century America* (Chapel Hill: University of North Carolina Press, 1959), 152.
13. Ibid.
14. Cotton Mather, quoted in David Levin, "Essays to Do Good for the Glory of God: Cotton Mather's Bonifacius," in *The American Puritan Imagination: Essays in Revaluation,* ed. Sacvan Bercovitch (Cambridge: Cambridge University Press, 1974).
15. Ibid., 143–44.
16. "The principle requires liberty of tastes and pursuits; of framing the plan of our life to suit our own character; of doing as we like, subject to such consequences as may follow: without impediment from our fellow creatures, so long as what we do does not harm them, even though they should think our conduct foolish, perverse or wrong." John Stuart Mill, *On Liberty,* ed. David Spitz (New York: Norton Books, 1975), 14.
17. "But neither one person, nor any number of persons, is warranted in saying to another human creature of ripe years, that he shall not do with his life for his own benefit what he chooses to do with it. He is the person most interested in his own well-being while, with respect to his own feelings and circumstances, the most ordinary man or woman has means of knowledge measurably surpassing those that can be possessed by anyone else." Ibid.
18. Derrick Bell, "The Price and Pain of Racial Perspective," in *The Law and Higher Education: Cases and Materials on Colleges in Court Durham, North Carolina,* ed. Michael Olivas (Durham, N.C.: Carolina Academic Press, 1989), 1038.
19. Ibid., 1038.

NOTES TO CHAPTER EIGHT

1. Kolb, "Learning Styles"; Hutchings and Wutzdorff, "Experiential Learning across the Curriculum," 5–19.

2. Horace Mann Bond, "Intelligence Tests and Propaganda: The Crisis (1924)," in *A Documentary History of The Negro People in the United States: 1910–1932*, ed. Herbert Aptheker, vol. 3 (New York: Citidal Press Book—Carol Publishing Group, 1990), 453.

3. Louise Erdrich, *Tracks* (New York: Harper and Row, 1989).

4. Gregory Bateson, *Steps to an Ecology of Mind* (New York: Ballantine Books, 1972).

5. Joe L. Kincheloe and Shirley R. Steinberg, "A Tentative Description of Post Formal Thinking: The Critical Confrontation with Cognitive Theory," *Harv. Educ. Rev.* 63 (1993): 296–316.

6. Gary Zukav, *The Dancing Wu Li Masters: An Overview of the New Physics* (New York: Harrow, 1979).

7. A. S. Byatt, *Still Life: A Novel* (New York: Macmillan, 1985).

8. Johnathan Culler, *The Pursuit of Signs: Semiotics, Literature, Deconstruction* (Ithaca: Cornell University Press, 1981).

9. Ibid., 191.

10. Valerie Walkerdine, *The Mastery of Reason: Cognitive Development and the Production of Rationality* (New York: Routledge, 1990).

11. Ibid., 190.

12. Howard Gardner, *Multiple Intelligences: The Theory in Practice* (New York: Basic, Division of Harper Collins, 1993).

13. Mary Catherine Bateson, *Composing a Life* (New York: Penguin Books, 1990).

14. See the discussion of the history of standardized testing and the growth of the ETS in David Owen, *None of the Above: Behind the Myth of Scholastic Aptitude* (Boston: Houghton Mifflin Company, 1985).

   Of particular interest is the discussion of the roots of educational testing in principles of eugenics and the confusion about what the test measures. Even though the ETS has tried to distance itself from its history and from the misuse of test scores, it has been singularly unsuccessful in convincing the lay public that the tests are not a measure of intellectual ability. Most of us assume that when a test purports to measure "higher order reasoning abilities," it is making a claim with respect to its ability to measure intelligence. Ibid., 201. For a discussion of the LSAT and the racial and gender bias in that examination, see Leslie Espinoza, "The LSAT: Narratives and Bias," *Am. U. J. Gender L.* 1 (spring 1993).

15. Among the worst offenders when it comes to test scores are law firms and investment banking firms. Owen, *None of the Above,* appendix B.
16. Perry, "Cognitive and Ethical Growth," 106.
17. L. Lee Knefelkamp, *Four Developmental Instruction Variables* (1981).
18. Perry, "Cognitive and Ethical Growth," 109.
19. James R. Elkins, "Writing Our Lives: Making Introspective Writing a Part of Legal Education," *Willamette L. Rev.* 29 (1993): 45.
20. Paul T. Wangerin, "Objective, Multiplistic, and Relative Truth in Developmental Psychology and Legal Education," *Tul. L. Rev.* 62 (1988). See also Angela P. Harris and Marjorie M. Shultz, "A(nother) Critique of Pure Reason: Toward a Civic Virtue in Legal Education," *Stan. L. Rev.* 45 (1993).
21. McLaren, *Schooling,* at 258.
22. Harmon, "Fragments on the Death Watch," 1.
23. The metaphor of teacher as midwife appears in the chapter titled "Connected Teaching" in Mary Field Belenky, Blythe McVicker Clinchy, Nancy Rule Goldberger, and Jill Matluck Tarule, *Women's Ways of Knowing: The Development of Self, Voice, and Mind* (New York: Basic Books, 1989). It was adapted to the law school setting in Barbara Bennet Woodhouse, "Mad Midwifery: Bringing Theory, Doctrine and Practice to Life," *Mich. L. Rev.* 91 (1993): 1977 in a rejoinder to the criticism of the impractical scholar by Judge Harry Edwards.

The idea is that it is good for us to "think out loud" so that our students will "see" the cognitive process by which we solve problems. Belenky et al., 217–19. Nor do I disagree with the critique of male models of moral development that have been offered by feminists like Belenky and Clinchy as well as Gilligan.

See a discussion of this critique in Wangerin, "Objective, Multiplistic, and Relative Truth," 1292–99.

24. McLaren, *Schooling,* 236.

25. See, e.g., the description of the role of the "liminal servant" in McLaren, which is to "imply the reinstatement of the charismatic character of the teacher and the power of intimacy and liminality." Ibid., 235.

26. McLaren, *Schooling,* 169.

27. Ibid.

28. The section of the MacCrate Report that touches on the duty of lawyers or practitioners to law students falls under the category "Fundamental Values of the Profession," and this section lists three ways in which attorneys should strive to improve the profession. The duty to "assist in the enterprise of educating new lawyers and preparing them for practice" is completely unstructured. Attorneys are advised that they can participate in "mentor and buddy systems" sponsored by state and local bar associations, training the young lawyers in their own firms, or preparing materials or lecturing in workshops for new lawyers. MacCrate Report, 210. None of this is obligatory, of course.

29. Knefelkamp, *Community of Scholars.*

30. Giroux, *Teachers as Intellectuals,* 126.

31. See discussion of Chinua Achebe's Anthills of the Savanah in Cheryl Harris "Law Professors of Color and the Academy: of Poets and Kings," *Chi.-Kent L. Rev.* 68 (1992): 332.

32. Richard A. Epstein, "Legal Education and the Politics of Exclusion," *Stan. L. Rev.* 45 (1993): 1607.

33. Elkins, *"Writing Our Lives".*

34. Ibid., 56–61.

35. For a discussion of the effect of law school on creativity see David R. Culp, "Law School: A Mortuary for Poets and Moral Reason," *Campbell L. Rev.* 16 (1994).

36. David Bohm and F. David Peat, *Science, Order, Creativity* (New York: Bantam Books, 1987), 104.

37. MacLeish, "Apologia," 1507.

38. MacLeish, "Apologia," 1510.

39. Ibid.

INDEX

225